ALSO BY ELEANOR CRAIG

One, Two, Three: The Story of Matt, a Feral Child

P.S. Your Not Listening

If We Could Hear the Grass Grow

ELEANOR CRAIG

SIMON AND SCHUSTER

NEW YORK

SIMON AND SCHUSTER and colophon are registered trademarks of Simon & Schuster
Designed by Eve Kirch
Manufactured in the United States of America

1   3   5   7   9   10   8   6   4   2

Library of Congress Cataloging in Publication Data
Craig, Eleanor.
If we could hear the grass grow.
1. Mentally ill children—Recreation.   2. Camps
for mentally ill children.   I. Title.
RJ505.R36C73   1983   618.92′891653   82-19691
ISBN 0-671-46188-5

This is a true story. The names of certain characters
have been changed to protect their privacy.

To Paul Richard Green

*With best wishes to
the children who came to Camp Hopewell,
their families and foster families,
their teachers and social workers,
and with special thanks to Fred Hills, editor,
and Don Congdon, literary agent.*

If We Could Hear
the Grass Grow

1

"You want a kid to die?" The pale, doughy boy was screaming at his mother. "Is that what you want? You want a kid to die?"

Mrs. Cassone had spent half an hour pleading with Frankie to get out of the car. When he finally did, it was to bolt across the yard and cower behind the wooden toilet cabinet the rental company had left at the entrance to the driveway.

"No, Frankie, I don't want you to die." His mother walked stiffly in the direction of her thirteen-year-old son.

I stood in the shadows on the left side of the porch, leaning against the railing, determined not to interfere. Instead, I glanced anxiously around my yard. Over fifty people—twice the number I had expected—had arrived this balmy morning to see the property I hoped to convert to a summer day camp for troubled children.

Some stood huddled in small clusters. Dave, my friend and fellow clinician, was showing others the interior of the barn. Many parents and children willingly took Dave's tour, but I was more aware of those who wouldn't.

Frankie leapt from behind the cabinet to pounce on his mother's slender shoulders.

"Then don't you ever leave me!" he shrieked. "I'll die if you leave me. Understand?" Grabbing both her arms he shook the pale woman so violently that her head bobbed uncontrollably. She closed her eyes but tears were already coursing down her deeply lined cheeks.

"Do you? Do you understand?" He shook her till her hairpins flew and her long tightly-knotted silk-red hair—the color of the boy's— spilled down her neck. "I'll die if you leave me!"

"Take your hands off me, Frankie." Her voice was flat. "I promise"—she swayed as though she might faint—"I promise I'll come here with you. I'll come to this camp every day until you're ready to stay alone—"

"NEVER!" His face contorted. "That's when I'll be ready— NEVER!" He spat in his mother's face. "I'll never be ready for you to leave me. Do you hear that? DO YOU?"

She stared at him with dull amber eyes, then wiped his saliva from her cheeks. Her hand trembled.

I wondered how Mrs. Cassone could have borne this so long. For three years Frankie had refused to go to school, refused to let his mother out of his sight. How could she have let that happen? And how could I, who'd never even been to day camp myself, imagine I could run one for kids as difficult as this?

Every spring, part of my job as a family counselor at the Child Guidance Clinic was to match the boys and girls who came to us for treatment with the right summer program.

I'd tried them all. The YMCA, recreation centers, wilderness camps. Invariably our kids could last through a "honeymoon" period of several days before succumbing to the incapacitating fears that kept them acting wild and angry or too intimidated to leave their homes, the behavior that brought them to us in the first place. The year before, one boy was sent home by taxi, fifty miles across the state, hours after he'd arrived at camp. So I knew only too well that troubled children had to have a special program.

Other summers I'd chosen to spend the time with my family and hadn't become so involved, but my life was different now, and I looked forward to becoming engrossed in this special summer project. Today would be a chance for me to meet potential campers and their parents and to assess my embryonic plans.

Dave had waved to Frankie's mother, inviting her to tour the barn. For every step she took in his direction, her son grabbed the bedraggled woman's hair or clothing to jerk her back to his side.

"Let go of me, son," she murmured. "I want to look around."

"No! No, Ma! Don't go! Don't leave me!" He yanked her sleeve so violently her blouse tore at the shoulder.

I felt a surge of compassion for the weary woman and for all the other adults who'd brought children to my home. Such a disparate collection, yet a common tension charged the air.

A sun-bronzed young couple in dazzling tennis whites chatted with another parent. But the woman in white was distracted and her eyes wandered off to the azalea bushes that flanked our cellar door. Moving closer to the foliage, I saw hiding under it a frail and serious-looking boy whose thick-lensed glasses lent him an owlish appearance. Each time his mother beckoned to him the boy backed deeper under the shrubs.

A tall, slim, blond girl, about thirteen, sat on the flagstone terrace, periodically moaning and clutching her stomach. This behavior clearly angered her look-alike mother, who tried to prod the girl with her brightly striped high-heeled sandal.

Near them, Adam, the gaunt wild-eyed boy I'd seen twice before at the clinic, paced endlessly along a stretch of driveway, mouthing words and flapping his arms like a bird, just as he had done in my office. His middle-aged aunt and uncle pleaded with him to stop. They had been appointed guardians by the court while his mother was confined to a mental hospital.

Eleven-year-old Gail, also a client of mine at the clinic, stood by the pool sucking her thumb and clinging to a fistful of her foster mother's skirt.

"*Señora!*" The call came from outside the fence near the road. A short, dark, heavily pregnant young woman in a flowered cotton housedress wearily pushed a squeaky stroller through the gate. Two sleeping babies, one about eighteen months, the other less than a year, shared the single carriage.

Three other children followed, all with skin the color of creamy coffee, round black eyes and dark curly hair like their mother's. The oldest boy was tall and slim; the second, a head shorter than his brother and even thinner. The delicate little girl wore a flowered dress of the same cloth as her mother's. Both dresses were freshly pressed but the colors had faded into soft pastel splotches.

I felt touched by the young mother, who introduced herself as

Angelina Hernandez, and by the dignity with which each of her children shook my hand. But they had, she told me, walked two miles to let me know the children couldn't come to camp as Dr. Bialek had suggested. The psychiatrist, medical director of the clinic, was treating their father with lithium and psychotherapy for manic-depressive reaction. "The children ride an emotional roller-coaster with this man," he'd said. "They need to be away from him as much as possible."

His final comment, "And they don't have any money," had prompted me to write to the local thrift shop, the Lion's Club and the Child Care Council, asking for a scholarship fund. Each group responded with a contribution.

"Why aren't they coming?" I asked, as the three older children clustered nearer their mother.

She kept her gaze on the babies. "This morning, this morning their father say to me, 'how I gonna pay some kinda camp for José and Carlos and Maria when we don't got no money for nothing?' "

As she spoke, I felt three pairs of round dark eyes searching mine.

"Only twenty-eight year old, my husband," she continued. "Too sick, he say, to go to work no more." She paused to stroke her great round belly. "Maybe—maybe next year somethin' gonna be better . . ."

The older boy muttered, "Doubt it," and kicked a clump of grass with the toe of his threadbare sneaker. The younger ones looked wistfully toward the pool.

"Mrs. Hernandez"—I touched her lightly—"I thought that Dr. Bialek told you, we have a scholarship fund to pay for your family."

The children looked anxiously from me to their mother.

"Your husband doesn't have to pay."

"Every morning," she said as the children watched her guardedly, "every morning I pray, 'Blessed Virgin Mother take care of my children.' This day, this day," she said, folding her hands and looking toward the sky, "Blessed Virgin Mary hear my prayer—"

"Yeah! Hooray!" The boys cheered and the little girl hugged her mother.

Just then a glossy purple bike careened into the driveway and squealed to a halt. The rider, a tall, muscular black boy, straddled the bike with his arms folded arrogantly across his chest. "Never fear," he shouted, brushing the front of his bright blue T-shirt embossed with a picture of the Fonz, "Never fear, the Big Man's here!"

Conversations across the sunny lawn came to a startled halt.

He turned to the Hernandez family. "C'mere," he beckoned, "give you all a look for one cheese enchilada."

The children edged behind their mother, whose eyes had suddenly hardened.

"No, no, *Señora.*" Big Man grinned in spite of her reacton. "I was only kiddin'. Let your kids come see my wheels. I don't charge nothin'—"

José backed further away. Maria spread both hands across her eyes. But Carlos, at ten the younger brother, approached the bike with reverence, and knelt to touch one gleaming spoke.

"Listen kid"—the biker's tone was confidential—"you don't always hafta call me Big Man. Rodney's the name." He thrust out his hand to Carlos. "Biking's my game."

Oh-oh. Bet it's not your only game, I found myself thinking.

"Hey look!" From the poolside, the black girl who'd been sucking her thumb commanded everyone's attention. "Lookit the baby robot!" she yelled, pointing up the driveway.

Heads swiveled to view a young couple, husband in business suit and tie, wife in a light blue dress, and between them their son, whose too-large skull was encased in a plastic helmet. The stunted child began each step by swinging a stubby leg sideways and then forward, creating the awkward rocking gait of a robot.

So this was Skipper. I remembered the call from his pediatrician. At nine Skipper had never been with a group of other children. He'd started life so alert and developed well for two years before the onset of his rare and progressive genetic disease. And now he was slowly dying.

I was startled by the way he looked. Surely a camp for troubled children, who were so prone to inflicting their own pain on others, was no place for this severely handicapped boy.

I went to greet them. I bent to eye level with the boy and smiled. "Hi, Skipper," I said, and his flattened features broke into a wrinkled but wonderfully contagious grin.

Someone in the back yard snickered. Then a call from Mrs. Hernandez mercifully drew the attention from Skipper and his parents. *"Ay caramba! Quitate!"* she cried. Both her babies were howling. An enormous bee circled round and round their stroller. "Go!" Their mother waved frantically. *"Largate!"*

"I'm coming." Rodney grabbed a baseball bat from the basket of his bike. "Don't worry, little kids, I'm coming!" He swatted recklessly till the bee was stunned and fell to the ground. "Never fear"— he held up the bat like a trophy—"the bee master's here."

"Gracias," the woman murmured. Rodney picked the dead bee up by his wings and winked at me.

With Skipper's appearance, all the children we expected had arrived. Dave, noticing my nervousness, quietly told me the morning was going well and helped me gather parents together for their instructions: Every child should bring his lunch, a bathing suit and towel. Parents must attend our weekly meetings, Thursday evenings at seven-thirty, in David's downtown office. And of course, for legal reasons, each camper must have signed permission in order to use the pool. If anyone had allergies—

"What's going on—" Dave held up his hand for me to stop talking and tilted his head to listen.

One of the women broke from the group and ran down the driveway screaming, "My God! My God! There's a child in the pool!"

Everyone scrambled from the porch, David leading the way. My nightmare had become a reality before camp had even begun!

Don't let him drown, don't let him drown—the words raced through my head as I tore across the yard.

At the edge of the pool Dave kicked off his sneakers, then dove in fully clothed. Moments later he emerged, climbing slowly up the ladder, both hands locked around the legs of a motionless boy whose bare bottom glistened above Dave's shoulder. The boy's head and arms dangled down against Dave's back.

"Adam!" his aunt cried. "Oh my God, it's Adam!" Slowly, almost imperceptibly, the boy began to squirm. Yes, he was definitely moving. I trembled with relief.

Then, suddenly he began to pound both fists against the seat of David's sopping pants. "Release me now, you foolhardy foe! Release me now or I'll whirl this water windward—"

The bare skin was too slippery to hold. Adam wriggled from Dave's grasp and bolted toward the road, a group of adults in close pursuit.

Dave caught him just as Big Man called out, "Man, oh man! You hear that honky talk?" He sounded like a ringmaster in the circus. "You folks all hear that crazy honky talk?"

I left Adam writhing on the ground, struggling against his uncle's effort to pin him down so his aunt could wriggle underpants over his flailing feet.

I walked past the father in white tennis clothes, who was crawling on his hands and knees into the bushes, calling to his son. Nearby, Frankie, from a running start, was ramming his head against the middle of his mother's back, screaming, "Take me home! I wanna go home!" The woman finally lost her balance and staggered toward the ground.

A babble of softly modulated voices drew my attention to the fence in front of the house. Horrified, I watched the real estate broker, a friend of my former husband's, unhook the latch on our gate and hold it for a well-dressed gray-haired couple.

The woman gasped. The man's eyes darted wildly from one child to another. The broker quickly fixed his gaze on the big white portable toilet with "W.C." painted boldly on its battered door.

"Wh—what's that?" He pointed, purplish splotches blooming on his neck.

But I had no chance to explain. Frankie had scurried back into his mother's car and was leaning out the window. "I hate your stinkin' guts, you wicked crazy lady," he yelled. "And I'm never comin' back to this rotten nutty camp!"

"Is that what's going on here?" the broker sputtered. "You think you're running a camp? On property you've been ordered to sell?"

"Just for eight weeks—"

"The judge will hear about this!" Red-faced and clucking angrily, he led his clients away.

The morning had ended in a total shambles. How could I, or anyone who came here, believe that I could handle those kids?

That night, long after the sun set behind the meadow across the street, I sat in a chipped green rocker on our old Victorian porch, wondering what to do. Hard to give up the dream of running my own program after eight years teaching in public schools and nine years as a therapist at the clinic. But maybe I should simply get on with moving and forget about a summer camp.

I thought back over my divorce and the court order stipulating that the house must be sold so the proceeds could be divided between my former husband and me. I had stuffed the car with empty cartons every time I returned from the store, until piles of boxes filled half the porch. But I had never brought one inside. Mentally I was far from ready to pack away the past, the hope that some day my children would bring our grandchildren to this home, and my secret dream that this house could also be a home for troubled kids who couldn't live with their families. Perhaps some of my own children would have helped me run it.

It was nearly a year since my own four children, hurt and confused by changes that to them appeared abrupt, had left home. It was not their going, but the way we managed to avoid each other before they left—even fixing meals at different hours—that haunted me later. Attempts to eat together served as reminders of earlier boisterous family gatherings and only increased the awkward silence.

It pained me to remember the uncharacteristic bitterness of Bill, my younger son, when he'd left the house in July, two days before his eighteenth birthday, saying I'd become a stranger in his eyes. Angered and bewildered by the divorce, Bill was protective and concerned about his father, and went to visit him at a writers' colony in New Hampshire. Two months later, Bill settled in Boston to work and go to school without calling or visiting me. When I phoned him he let me know he wasn't ready for us to talk.

Two months after Bill left, I drove Richard, twenty-two, to Boston, where he had a one-year appointment as a substitute teacher. The trip afforded three private hours to talk. At first we used the time to ruminate about the past.

But when we stopped for hot dogs at a Howard Johnson's we began to talk about his future—how disappointing it was to graduate from college eager to teach and find only substitute positions. "I can't afford to live that way for long, but it ought to get me by while I figure out what's next." Rich said.

We untied the mattress from the station wagon roof and hauled the bed, the stereo, his drums, clothes and books up the darkened stairway to his small apartment.

As he leaned into the car to say goodbye, I looked at my adult son's gleaming black hair and mustache, more reminiscent of my mother's Spanish background than of the Craig or O'Brien sides of the family. He smiled crookedly at me.

"Look, Ma, if—when—the house sells, I'd like plenty of warning so I can get the rest of my books and records. Okay?"

We kissed through the open window. "Take care now, Ma—" his voice was choked.

I knew the move for Richard was a positive one. For me, at that moment, it felt like one more loss.

Ellen was less able than Richard to talk about the changes. At seventeen, the youngest of the four, she felt our family problems even more acutely because of the natural turmoil of adolescence. Her way of adapting was to present a cool reserve, a misleading unresponsiveness about herself.

The exuberant girl whose long auburn hair once blew around her delicate oval face as she danced and rode horseback became a subdued young woman with serious eyes, her lovely hair confined in a bun.

I knew she was sharing confidences with a boy she'd met in high school, but safe conversation with me remained focused on which art course she'd take and what I should feed our aging dog, Millie, while she was away at college.

I hoped her new experiences at school, away from family stresses, would be happy ones. But soon after she moved to campus, about fifty miles from home, Ellen began to call.

She had little in common with the carefree freshmen in her dorm. Be more involved, less sensitive, I urged her. But the frequent calls left no doubt that dormitory life was really hard for Ellen.

Ann was last to leave. Off on an extensive trip with a classmate from Brown, she planned a comparative study of contemporary religious cults along the East Coast of Africa. We had talked as I helped her put malaria tablets into her backpack and stuff the royal blue sleeping bag into its cylindrical nylon case.

Watching her, her blue eyes and long brown hair so like mine and my mother's before me, I thought how different my life had been at her age. Early marriage, pregnancies, no dreams of exploration. Yet while I admired her courage and independence, I felt uneasy about her traveling now—a sense that she was fleeing.

"Ann—there's so much I'd like to say. You seem more distant than you ever used to be . . ."

She stiffened, then sat beside me on the edge of the bed. "Look, Ma, you've got to understand what's going on with me has nothing to do with the divorce." Head bowed, her speech became hesitant. "I—ah—I just haven't really felt—ah—happy for—for a long time. Something's wrong . . . I don't know what. Please don't worry, Ma." She looked up but her eyes were remote. "I'm sure this trip will help."

I saw her off at the Bridgeport railroad station. Ann was taking a train to Montreal and from there a charter flight to Cairo. She looked too young and frail for the heavy pack she carried on her back.

Long after the train was out of sight I found myself still waving, straining for a last glimpse of my oldest child's pale face.

At home I unlocked the door, then stood on the darkened porch of our empty yellow house to relive a simple game we'd played returning from trips at night when the children were little.

"What's the best part about going away?" their father would ask, always fumbling for the key.

"Coming back home!" all four would scream, and they'd scramble inside. I walked up the stairs in the empty house without turning on a light.

Throughout that fall and winter my work at the Clinic became an escape that served me well. I scheduled every hour, leaving no time during the day without appointments. And I came to realize that the suffering we had experienced in our own family enabled me to become a more effective family therapist.

Alone at night I could hardly sleep, and spent night after night wandering through each room, trying to reconstruct details of the conflicts in my marriage I had so dimly perceived and so overtly denied. No holiday, no well-meant invitation, could distract me.

Weekends I filled by attending professional meetings, ostensibly so I could learn new skills, although privately, I knew that I was looking for help. I kept myself geared into an almost impossible schedule, until early March. Finally, as the ice and snow were melting, I reached the point where I no longer had to keep so frantically busy. At last I could sleep through the night. Rested, I felt my energy return. Each day I saw more clearly what I wanted. To have a day camp for troubled children. And spend one last summer with my children in this house. A final chance to reweave more smoothly the family ties that bound us. Then I ought to be ready to move.

For now I wanted time with Ann, Richard, Bill and Ellen—not for marathon rap sessions, but time for us to share as adults, for them to experience my work, to know me. We could run the camp together.

Early in April I wrote out the details to each of them, changing the wording so many times that the final copy began to read like the first. It ought to work, I told myself as I walked downtown to mail the letters, for our family, just beginning to heal, to be reaching out to others. The give and take should help us all.

But my children had gone to begin their own lives, relieved, perhaps, to leave a home that had so radically changed. I wondered which, if any, would be willing to return.

2

In the beginning Dave tried to talk me out of having the camp at my home.

His stories about accidents and liability scared me into asking several ministers and the director of a long-established camp if they had space to rent. Their answers left no doubt about it; if it wasn't at my home, there'd be no camp at all.

"I hope you've got a certified lifeguard," Dave ventured next.

I hadn't thought about that.

"Hey, Eleanor." He shook his head. "You could really be in trouble. Not one kid should put a toe in your pool until you have that protection. And," he paused melodramatically, then grinned, "it just so happens you're looking at a Red Cross certified lifeguard—"

"Uh-uh. Can't afford you."

"Damn right, you can't!" He laughed. "But I'm a volunteer! I'm cutting time at the clinic to start a private practice, but it's your good luck to catch me in-between, before the crowds line up at my door."

Dave was great with kids, and he'd been kind to me, but I didn't know him well and felt uncomfortable accepting such a generous offer. However, he was insistent and in the end I accepted.

Our first task was reviewing the work I'd done on the budget. This camp was not intended to be a money-making venture. I'd juggle my clinical hours to afternoons and evenings to ensure my regular income.

If my children would work as counselors, I wanted to pay them each seventy-five dollars weekly. They could earn more in other, less pressured summer jobs. Dave and I figured that to cover salaries, plus food and supplies, we'd have to charge thirty-five dollars a week per child. We knew some parents couldn't afford it and struggled to distribute the donations we'd been given as fairly as possible.

It was fun to share the dream with Dave, and have his help with the planning. Sometimes we argued over the program—how much structure or flexibility these children needed. But we were both working on the premise that troubled children come from troubled families, and we both had strong commitments to working with the whole family when one child had been singled out as the "problem."

I'd rarely seen troubled kids make lasting gains unless their parents made changes also. Most of these children become scapegoats who, like mirrors, reflect and magnify unresolved conflicts at home.

So often our work with families of troubled children shifted to marital counseling or intensive help for the single parent, helping adults come to terms with the limitations of their own parents, forgiving what they did and failed to do for them as children. Remembering almost-forgotten conflicts that had long been submerged but never disappeared, festering instead to disrupt the parenting for yet another generation.

Dave and I wanted very much to include in the program frequent meetings with each camper's family, but we realized we'd have no time for that. We finally had to settle for a much more limited goal—a happy summer vacation for kids who might not find one elsewhere.

We had decided to invite potential campers to visiting day—the day that seemed such a mockery of the ordered yet nurturing environment I hoped to offer.

I sat on the porch for hours that night, trying to rock away my sense of futility. At midnight I finally went upstairs, still undecided about going ahead with the camp.

It took about a week before I could laugh at David's recapitulation of that morning. But by then I'd already begun to schedule in appointments with as many children and parents as I could see before the end of June. In spite of my doubts, there would be a camp this summer.

3

Although she was only five feet tall, Gail was overweight and clearly beginning to develop breasts. Her hair was separated into rows of tiny braids, and her skin was darker and more lustrous than her foster parents'.

She dominated our meeting by stretching out on the couch between her foster parents, her head on Mrs. Bennett's lap, her feet pushing Mr. Bennett to the far end.

"My wife and I are both teachers." The bearded black man's voice was gentle. "Our two boys are off at college, and the oldest one just got married. We took in Gail, hoping we can help her. Because"—he looked directly at the girl—"I know what it means to get bounced around. I was raised in eight different foster homes myself—"

Although he was choking with emotion, Gail ignored her foster father. Instead her mischievous long-lashed eyes studied every inch of me, from the shell barrette that held my too-long hair to the bottom of my beige crepe-soled shoes.

"We want to offer her stability." Mrs. Bennett patted the girl's braided head. Gail shut her eyes and smiled. Deep dimples appeared in her cheeks. "We've even talked about adopting her, but Gail doesn't seem to want that—"

"Hey!" Gail suddenly sat up. "What kinda kids be comin' to your camp? They be good, I be good to them. But they be bad, I'm gonna kick a lotta people's butts in. Miss Bennett here"—she rolled her eyes toward her foster mother—"she tryin' to tell me fighting ain't for ladies. Well, that ain't what my real mother tole us. She be fighting all the time with all her boyfriends. And she said, 'beat on any kid that gives you trouble.' She says, 'try your best to kill them.' "

I shook my head. "We have different rules at Camp Hopewell."

The silence of Diane, who came in next, was a jarring contrast to Gail's verbosity. The fourteen-year-old girl and her mother looked like Scandinavian models—both blond, blue eyed and high-cheek-boned. But Mrs. Woodruff wore a white silk blouse and crisply pleated light beige pants. She strode in confidently. Diane, engulfed in a shapeless cardigan, shuffled along behind. The girl's back curved in a semi-circle. Both hands were clutched on her stomach.

When I asked the girl if her stomach hurt it was her mother who responded. "Diane's stomachaches are nerves, just nerves. All caused by her father, who blames me because Diane has been so difficult. He says that I don't give her enough attention and he wants her to stay with him in the city on weekends."

"How do you feel about that, Diane?" I asked, trying to see her face.

"Why should she object?" her mother snapped, tugging on the gold chains at her neckline. "He buys her off with clothes and dinners—"

The girl looked up long enough to mouth "fuck you" at her mother.

"What did you say?" The woman's face reddened.

"You're just jealous of me and Daddy," Diane muttered, her head bowed.

"That's ridiculous, Mrs. Craig," the woman sniffled. "I'm trying to protect my daughter. She doesn't understand her father's nasty methods. That's why I need a written statement from you saying that Diane shouldn't have to see her father."

When I said I couldn't make that judgment she remembered another appointment and whisked her daughter out of my office.

Before I saw them, I heard them fighting in the hallway.

"I never get to do what I want—"

"Listen, boy. No son of mine gonna spend his summer hangin' in that pool hall. Now get in that room before the lady think you don't wanna go to her camp."

"I don't give a shit what she think—"

The huge woman shoved her barrel-chested son across the door-way so forcefully he reeled across the carpet and crashed against the wall. He turned slowly and stooped to retrieve a big plastic comb from the floor and replaced it in the crown of his Afro hairdo. Then, leaning in the corner, one foot against the wall, he crossed his arms and glowered at his mother.

She sank into a cushioned chair, shaking her head. It was hard to connect this surly boy with the outgoing kid who had called himself Big Man and come alone on his bike to our visiting day. But I knew he had mood swings. Again and again the story appeared on his record: the kid who'd been most popular in his class also waited in the bathroom wielding scissors to coerce his fellow students into giv-ing him money.

"I don't know why"—the woman took an aqua tissue from the pocket of her bulky knit sweater and dabbed at her forehead—"I don't know why he act like he do."

"Why don't ya tell my father?" Rodney sneered. "Tell him about the money too."

His mother sighed and turned to me. "I'm ashamed to say it. My own son takin' money from my pocket to spend it down at that pool hall—"

The young man nodded in agreement. "Somebody got somethin' I want"—he swaggered, hands crammed into his skin tight jeans— "the old devil start urgin' on me to take it."

Suddenly he spun around on the toe of his pointed cowboy boots, to watch my reaction. "An' when that devil push on me, man, that's when Big Man here be gettin' into trouble." He pounded his chest.

I was loud and firm. "Rodney, it's not the devil I'll be watching in camp. It's you."

"Old sorrow put a cross on my back," his mother moaned, "the day his father left me to raise this boy alone."

With those words, Rodney suddenly changed. He sank limply into the nearest chair, burrowed his head into his nylon jacket and pulled up the zipper to completely envelop his face.

"Where is your father?" I asked.

No response from Rodney.

"He been gone since Rodney was three. And ever since he been gone the boy been nothin' but evil. His two big sisters don't give me no trouble but if this one don't improve I can't keep him home with me no more. He tears me up too bad, tellin' me I hated his father and I got nothin' but hate for him. That ain't true, Miss Craig. But the boy won't let no one help him. And he won't never take them pills the doctor ordered—"

"Them pills—" Rodney's voice was muffled under the jacket. "Them pills"—he began to rock—"ain't never gonna calm me . . ."

"Kids always pick on me. I don't know why." The frail boy who'd hidden in the bushes had a high shrill voice. His thick-lensed horn-rimmed glasses and serious face made him look like a little professor.

"Tim's always alone." His mother's voice quavered. "No one in the neighborhood ever plays with him."

"How come?" I asked him. But his mother answered for him, her eyes bright with tears. "He never has had a friend. A child his age should have one friend . . ."

I put my hand beside my cheek to screen out his mother, and look directly at the boy. "What about that, Tim?" I asked him.

"It's because of my interest in paleontology—dinosaurs and prehistoric monsters. They all make fun of me. So I throw their baseballs into the pond whenever they hit them into our yard. Everybody hates me. They always did."

"Everybody?" I raised my eyebrows. "Are you sure?"

Tim nodded somberly. "Everybody," he repeated.

"Then you'll have to make a friend at camp," I said, "so it will be everybody minus one. I think I can help you do that, so I'm glad that you'll be coming . . ."

"I prefer to read in the summertime," Tim said. "It's what I've always done and I'd rather keep things the same. I don't want to come to your camp."

"I really wish you'd try it," his mother pleaded softly. Tim's mother answered the questions I asked her son, but let him make decisions that were meant for her.

"No," I interrupted. "You said Tim needs a friend, more than he needs a summer of isolation. Sometimes kids need help knowing what's really best for them. It's got to be your decision, Mrs. McNulty, not your son's."

．．．

"I'm Laura's mother," the gray-haired woman said, leading her husband into the office. Their three older children, two boys and a girl, all in late teens or early twenties, shuffled by me, looking embarrassed, mumbling responses to my greetings.

Laura, frail and thin, younger in appearance than eleven, moved haltingly across the room, her left foot toeing in at ninety degrees, and wedged herself in between her parents on the couch, crossed her arms and glared defiantly at her siblings.

"I don't know why we had to come." The older brother returned her stare. "That kid's the one with the problems—"

"Don't start that again!" his mother commanded. The girl began to wail. Her mother wrapped her in her arms and pulled her closer to her large round bosom. Sniffling, Laura stuck out her tongue at her brother.

"Laura will be out of camp for at least a week." Mrs. Burgman stroked her daughter's dark blond hair, and the girl's brown eyes peered through wispy bangs to fasten on her mother's. "She'll be at Children's Hospital for an operation."

"What will the doctor do?" I asked Laura, who burrowed closer to her mother. Her brother sighed in disgust. "Her leg is the least of that kid's problems," he muttered, but refused to say more.

"They'll release the tendons at the knee and ankle," her mother answered, glaring at her son. "When Laura returns to camp her leg will be in a cast. She won't be able to swim."

"When's the operation, Mr. Burgman?" I turned to her father.

"They'll let us know," his wife answered. "Whenever a room becomes available."

The spindly girl twirled several strands of hair around her index finger.

"Stop it, Laura!" Her mother grabbed her arm. "That's how you've pulled out all your hair before! The child was almost bald the first time we came here to see the doctor."

Slouching, her balding husband never looked up. "Alopecia," he said, labeling his daughter's condition. He continued to twist a metal key chain round and round his thumb.

．．．

When I saw nine-year-old Skipper again, without the distractions we'd had on visiting day, I had even graver doubts about his coming to camp.

The size of a four-year-old, he waddled into the room supported by his anxious parents, wearing the same plastic helmet.

"You know about his condition—an enzyme deficiency that didn't show up until he was two." Mr. Kerrigan kept his eyes on his son, who played with blocks on the floor. "Till then we thought he was brighter than his sisters. Now he hardly says a word. We—ah—we sent you the reports."

"I read them," I nodded, "but I'm worried about how the other kids will be with Skipper."

"Please," his mother said, inching to the edge of her chair, "please. He's got to have a chance to be with other children. We couldn't find another place to take him close enough to home—"

"My wife"—her husband cleared his throat—"my wife needs a break. She's only thirty-one, but she says she feels like she's ancient. We've finally both decided Skipper's got to have a life of his own. And so do we. If he does well this summer, we'll find a special school for him in September. We're ready for Skipper to have as full a life as he can—for just as long as he's able. We realize there are risks . . . but we"—he leaned closer toward me—"we need some time to breathe."

Rocking, humming a low steady monotone, Skipper was lost within his plastic universe.

Mrs. Cassone, whose son had torn her blouse on visiting day, called to cancel their appointment at the very moment I expected them. Frankie's heart was racing. He had a stomachache too. No, she couldn't bring him. No, she couldn't possibly come alone.

I hung up, disappointed and angry. We were seeing more and more kids like Frankie at the clinic—ostensibly school-phobic, in fact afraid to leave their mothers. All with stomachaches, sore throats or palpitations. Their teachers yelled, the children complained. The other kids were mean. And the lonely mothers, as much afraid of separation as the children, chose to believe and repeat their excuses, allowing their offspring to become their jailers. Such "good mothers" existed with no hope of having lives of their own. Their children's anxiety provided an endless excuse to live without facing their own fears.

Frankie, like the others, had begun with daily trips to the nurse's office. Then a four-day absence triggered his refusal to go back to school. His worried mother took him to a psychiatrist who medicated the boy and told the school authorities Frankie was "too phobic" to return the rest of that school year. He'd need a tutor to teach him at home.

The recommendation was renewed year after year. Every single day he missed, every week, the gap between Frankie and his classmates widened. I could barely contain the fury I felt about such inadequate treatment.

I hoped that a small summer camp would provide children like Frankie a chance to socialize again—without the academic pressure of school.

Now I doubted that Frankie would make it. And there was an even greater disappointment. I still hadn't heard from my own son Bill, since I had sent the letter in April asking him to work with me for the summer.

I understood now why I had no answer from Ann. I'd written her at the only address she'd left, c/o American Express, Dar Es Salaam, Tanzania. But late in May, her long, vividly detailed letter arrived, telling of meetings with witch doctors in Nairobi, and being locked in a rented room in Uganda for her own protection. Breathtaking tales. No mention of when she would get to Tanzania.

Richard had called the night he'd received his letter. "A camp for troubled children? At our house—on Hopewell Road?" He laughed into the phone. "We won't let you forget this summer, Ma! Having a camp while you're trying to move oughta keep things hopping. I'll be there. But did I tell you, I'm applying for the Peace Corps? If I get accepted, I'll be leaving."

Ellen, the youngest, had come home on Memorial Day weekend to talk about what her job would be. She'd never taught art to kids before, but she was willing to try. She'd be home for good on June eighteenth.

Then on the sixth of June I found three sleeping bags on the porch.

Without warning, Bill had arrived, bringing two college friends to help him replace split boards in the barn and install a rebuilt motor to filter the pool. They had just finished their final exams, and seemed surprised not to be expected.

Billy's friends slept on the porch until they found a nearby apartment. They were pleasant and hard working. But they also served as buffers. I rarely saw Billy alone.

Yet it was he who named the camp after the road we lived on. And he who drew up the flyer announcing the dates, the hours and the goals of Camp Hopewell.

CAMP HOPEWELL
A summer program for children with special needs
Ages 6–13
July 5–August 20

Hopewell Camp is designed to meet the special needs of children with learning disabilities or emotional difficulties. Our goals are to enhance the camper's social adjustment through group activities while sharpening perceptual skills in a program of physical education, arts, and tutoring. Close cooperation with parents and school will ensure campers of highly individualized attention.

SPORTS
    Swimming
    (senior lifesaver)
Dance and
    Creative Movement
Games
  and
    Yoga
TUTORING in
Reading and
    Language Arts

ART
    Painting   Clay
    Drawing

    Collage
    Puppets

    Papier Mâché
MUSIC
    Singing, Instruments
    and Band

Plus: Guest performers, a cookout, and more!!
Mon.–Fri. 9:30–3:00 $35 per week
Please call Eleanor Craig, Director, 555-1623

4

Richard and Ellen both arrived on June eighteenth, settled their belongings, revisited old high school friends and turned to helping Bill. While I was at the clinic, all three spent days cleaning and repairing the barn. They searched through closets and in the basement for sporting goods and games, set up a net for volleyball, laid out a baseball diamond.

Evenings they went out with friends. Since they'd been home I was sorry we'd found so little time to talk. Perhaps I had pressured them into coming back before they were really ready. Yet I was encouraged by their involvement in preparing for the camp, which was to start on the fifth of July.

Saturday, the third, we spent the day around our dining-room table going over schedules, first on a weekly basis then one day at a time. Each counselor would offer two activities every morning. Children would be free to choose and rotate.

Dave would supervise the pool and swim instruction. Rich, who loved all sports, was our athletic director. Bill would teach camp songs, play guitar, direct drama, games and quieter activities. Ellen was in charge of art—painting, crafts and work with clay.

My responsibility was for overall direction, tutoring in reading, group and individual help as needed, contact with the parents. Therapy would be informal. Every new skill, each successful social encounter would be therapeutic for these children.

We also talked about what to expect—the extremes of behavior our campers were bound to present—how one child expresses rage by lashing out and hurting other people while another deals with the very same feeling by turning the fury inward on himself, withdrawing from contact with others.

"You'll learn a lot about yourself," Dave assured them, "working with kids who'll challenge and defy you."

"I'm worried about fights," Ellen said, nervously fingering her silver ring. "What should we do to stop them?" I know she was thinking of the slammed doors, the angry words, in our own family.

"Think about it!" Dave tapped his forehead, smiling. "What do parents usually do when kids are fighting? They scream, they hit and they preach, but still nothing changes. So I've devised a method I like to call the positive element of surprise—" He leaned forward over the table, his voice intense. "You go up to the underdog, the less powerful kid in the fight, and take him away to do something completely different, leaving the other kid without a target. And both kids are astounded, because it's usually the aggressor who gets the attention."

"That sounds like avoiding the problem, Dave. I think we should come on straight with these kids." Bill turned to me, challenging. "What do you think, Ma?"

I was too confused to answer. Bill was normally soft-spoken, and I was surprised by the harshness in his tone. Suddenly, I felt the issue had switched from how to handle kids to having Dave become an authority in our house.

Dave was flushing. He had felt it also. I felt caught in the middle, an all too painful and familiar position.

"I like"—I groped for words—"to encourage kids to come up with their own solutions to their disagreements. But I trust your ability to handle trouble. Just one warning. Don't threaten to send kids home when they're misbehaving. We took them knowing that they all have problems. We're giving them a safe place to show us what they are."

In the second part of the meeting we talked about each of the children, beginning with Frankie. Dave summarized the history of his fears, beginning with his difficulty in kindergarten.

"How should we deal with a kid like that?" Ellen asked.

"Let's just start with a modest plan," Dave suggested. "A goal we can hope to achieve—just for Frank to come to camp daily. That's more than he's done at school in the past three years."

"Right on." Bill smiled appreciatively, breaking the tension between them. "I can go with that."

"What's with that girl?" Richard looked puzzled when we discussed Laura. "She made a great hit during the ball game, but the moment I told her so, she threw herself on the grass in a screaming fit."

"Be careful, Rich." Dave sounded more relaxed. "Praise for people who don't feel good about themselves can be a very threatening thing. It reminds me"—he sat back a moment deep in thought—"of hearing about concentration-camp survivors who died from eating when they finally got released. They couldn't handle food, although it was exactly what they needed."

Richard nodded. "So, small doses for a kid like Laura."

Ellen reviewed the description of Gail's life before she was placed in the Bennetts' home. "So she had all the responsibility when her mother was drinking. It was Gail who shopped and cooked and took care of four younger children." Ellen sounded troubled. "Then one night without any warning she's brought to a home where she's supposed to act like a happy little girl. No wonder she cried and fought with other kids. And now to be caught in a custody fight between the state and her mother."

When Dave mentioned Adam, Ellen said he was the weirdest boy she'd ever seen. "I felt really frightened."

"Some of his background might help you understand." Dave pulled Adam's psychological evaluation from his briefcase, and scanned the long report for the more descriptive sections.

"Reason for referral": he read aloud, "This twelve-year-old boy is being seen by the examiner as part of a diagnostic intake. He is currently living with his aunt and uncle while his mother is hospitalized for what her sister describes as a 'third schizophrenic break.' He had been placed in a special education class, but his teacher reported his bizarre behavior upsetting to the class. He was unable to remain seated, and unable to accomplish academic tasks. Attention span and concentration poor. The head social worker referred Adam to the Child Guidance Center for evaluation.

"Summary of personal history: No information about pregnancy, labor or delivery. Mother lived in commune where child was born. Aunt saw him at eighteen months and reports that he was walking, but no intelligible speech had developed. Mother was known to have taken L.S.D.

"Child and mother have lived in several communes in western Massachusetts and northern Vermont. Last known dwelling was a converted school bus mother shared with a twenty-five-year-old dishwasher. Recent X-rays indicated that child has had a broken arm and broken collarbone that have healed. His aunt states that she now believes her sister inflicted those injuries on her son. No reports were ever filed to support that suspicion." David paused, thoughtful for a moment.

"Behavioral observations: An awkward youngster just entering adolescence," he went on, "he evidences an array of nervous symptoms including hand motions, head jerking, inability to sit still and bursting out with loud inappropriate phrases in a kind of comic-book super-hero language. At times he is completely preoccupied with ruminations about power, action and violence. At other times Adam's behavior seems deliberately designed to test the examiner. For instance, he attempted to poke his finger into a fan. When warned, he proceeded to pretend again. One must consider that the implication of this act, carried through, is self-mutilation. His speech constantly refers to blood, fighting, destruction by fire.

"Intellectual functioning: On first appointment Adam's anxiety was too high for testing to proceed. On second sitting he measured in the borderline defective range. Later testing may determine whether anxiety has depressed his level of functioning. Results suggest the lag in cognitive development may be a reaction to his life experience.

"Summary: An extremely anxious twelve-year-old male exhibiting many signs of ego disturbance of functional origin, perhaps complicated by organic factors. We find he has themes of aggression and object loss. The mother figure is seen as attacking. This youngster deals with overwhelming feelings of helplessness by retreating into

fantasies of possessing super powers which enable him to control the
threatening world around him . . .

"Prognosis: Poor." Dave fell silent.

Bill had stopped taking notes long before Dave finished reading.
"I . . ." He had to clear his throat before he could continue. "I used
to wish for super powers too, when I was a kid."

I'd been thinking that, too, and my own voice sounded choked as I
responded. "I remember, Bill, all those Spiderman drawings of yours
we taped to the kitchen cupboards."

"That's what I like about working with these children," Dave said,
looking from Bill to me. "We've all known some of what they're
feeling. It's just a matter of degree. But Adam's in such tough shape I
think he may need more than he can get on an outpatient basis
alone."

Bill shook his head. "Maybe the camp will help him."

"I can't stop thinking of Gail," Ellen said softly. "With a background like that, what can we hope to offer her here?"

Richard was watching Ellen thoughtfully. "Maybe," he said to his
younger sister, "maybe we can give her back a little of her missing
childhood."

As one last item on the agenda, we tried to clarify what our goals
would be for each of the children:

- Rodney must get control of his temper . . .
- Tim should make a friend . . .
- Frankie had to separate from his mother . . .
- Laura would need support before and after her operation . . .
- Adam should be observed in terms of future planning . . .
- Diane needed to improve her poor self-image . . .
- The Hernandez children would be watched for signs of physical
  or emotional abuse . . .
- Skipper would be in a group for the first time . . .

Late in the afternoon Dave snapped the locks on his briefcase and
smiled at each of the serious faces before he left the table. "See you
Monday," he said, and paused in the doorway to give a thumbs-up
salute.

. . .

"What do you want for supper?" I asked Ellen. "How about a cookout?"

"No thanks, Mom. I'll be going out to dinner." She hurried up the stairs to change her clothes.

Richard packed up his drums, hugged me quickly and drove off to a practice.

"We're used to cooking for ourselves, Ma," Bill said gently when I tried to make suggestions.

At seven-thirty a bright blue van pulled into the driveway, and Bill jumped in with the two young men who'd stayed with us before they found an apartment. The house was quiet again, the way it had been all winter. I went upstairs with a book but the door to the attic prompted me to reconsider. Maybe there were still useful things up there for the camp.

5

At first I could hardly see. The naked overhead light bulb lengthened the shadows as I stooped to pull one box after another out from under the recessed eaves. By the time my eyes adjusted to the dimness I had forgotten my original purpose as carton by carton, layer by layer, I began to unearth the history of our family.

Ann and Richard's college yearbooks. A fraying photo of my mother in her beaded wedding gown and pointed satin shoes. Ellen's "Chatty Cathy" doll, Ann's collections of games, the punching bag clown, the H-O trains, the hockey set and Richard's planes. A dollhouse with one wall upside down I'd put together one Christmas Eve, a faded blackboard, cartons of books, baby shoes, grammar school awards, my first teaching certificate, a glossy picture of their father and me sipping piña coladas in a tropical nightclub.

I knelt by the cartons labeled FRAGILE to unwrap the paper toweling around a ceramic ashtray Richard had made in kindergarten, a clay guinea pig Billy had sculpted the day his real pet died. Then I came to the scrapbooks of reviews that heralded my former husband's books, and I began to read them once again.

I jumped at the soft patter of dog's paws on the attic stairs. Old Millie settled near me with a groan, returning me to the present. An aged book review lay crumbled in my hand. Gently I placed it back in the scrapbook. One of the children could return it to their father.

Late into the night I perched on the old metal trunk in the attic, unwrapping, repacking and remembering. It couldn't be accomplished quickly, this exploration of a family that had thrived for over two decades. But I was more focused now, more able to sort out the dolls, the jump ropes, the books and games that we could use with other children.

Long after midnight I carried two large cartons down the stairs. The old dog trailed me across the darkened yard to the barn.

6

Monday. The first day of Camp Hopewell. At five A.M. I found myself taking a final nervous tour of the yard, too tense to sleep any longer. Were we really ready to have eleven needy children here every weekday for eight weeks?

Barefoot and wearing my old blue bathrobe, I walked from the tall yellow farmhouse on the hill down the sloping driveway to our rambling rosy-beige barn. The rising sun blazed on the copper rooster that had perched on the cupola for over a hundred years. Below it, Richard had mounted a basketball net, just above the sliding wooden doors leading to the area Ellen had set up for art.

About fifty feet in front of the barn was the ten-year-old pool, surrounded by a flagstone terrace. I knelt to inspect the five big patches Billy had glued to the plastic liner, hoping they'd last the summer.

Farther down the gentle hill, behind the pool, Richard and Bill had cleared an acre of wildflowers and high grass to make a baseball diamond. Standing at home plate, I was flooded again with disturbing doubts. The yard was ready, but were we? Had I really prepared my children for the kind of kids I knew were coming? Had we bought enough supplies—paper, crayons, clay—the right equipment? Were activities well-planned and would the children be able to make choices, or should I have drawn up a more rigid schedule, as Dave had suggested?

Too nervous to stand still, I jogged around the bases Richard had marked with the old green cushions from the rockers on our porch. Twice around the field and I felt calmer. I enjoyed having dirt on my feet, like a kid, and it felt good to wipe them on the dewy morning grass.

Two final things left to do. Bring the telephone outside, through the basement window, in case of an emergency. Leave the first-aid kit by the pool.

Ellen and I were making lemonade to serve at lunch time. I'd already mixed in a can of frozen grapefruit juice by mistake, then added two extra cups of water, when Skipper's mother knocked on the kitchen door.

She looked so afraid to be leaving her son that my own nervousness vanished. Leaving the sticky fruit cans on the counter, I quickly wiped my hands and went to greet them. It took several moments of quiet reassurance that Skipper would be all right before she could let go of his hand.

Ellen lifted Skipper onto the kitchen stool while I walked his mother to the porch to say goodbye.

"Whatcha got in there?" Ellen tapped the metal lunch box. Under the dome of his plastic helmet Skipper's flattened features broke into a crinkly grin.

"Pee budder." He laughed, and so did she.

I put the pitchers of lemonade in the refrigerator while Ellen helped Skipper climb off the high stool. Getting down would have been an easy task for any six-year-old, and Skipper was nine, but not only was his body stunted, his legs were disproportionately short and his head too large and heavy for the blunted torso.

Ellen's first assignment was to collect all the lunches and designate spaces in the garage for each child's bathing suit and towel. I watched her guide Skipper, our first camper, down the outside stairs, her hand under his elbow, his body rocking from left to right each time he took a step.

Cars were pulling up in front. Excited, I ran outside to join Bill and Dave, who were waiting for the children at the gate.

Laura's mother called goodbye from the car, but the crippled girl loped awkwardly toward Bill and didn't respond, if she heard.

Adam leapt from his aunt's car before it rolled to a stop. "Kkpow! Kaablam! The time of the fiery phoenix has arrived!" Hands thrust before him, Adam bounded down the driveway and the towel around his bony shoulders flapped like a cape.

"Oh no!" Dave chased him. "No you don't! Not again!"

Dave caught the towel just as Adam started to dive. "You and I are holding hands a while, old pal."

Adam made harmless punching motions. "Pow! Zak! The decision has been taken from me! But Mr. Fantastic bears no malice."

Diane and her mother drove up in a cream-colored sports car, but the girl didn't get out. She was shaking her head, and Mrs. Woodruff looked angry. Suddenly she leapt from the driver's seat and dashed around the car to the door on her daughter's side. Diane was clinging to the seat belt like a life line when her mother pulled her out of the car.

Tim arrived, looked around furtively and dashed down the driveway. "I'll be home if you need me," his mother called. But he was already crawling under the azalea bush.

"My turn," Bill said, and he went after Tim just as Mrs. Cassone drove in with Frankie. I was pointing to the garage, telling her where Frank should put his clothes, when the boy streaked behind a wide-based maple tree, moving his pudgy body with surprising speed. His mother dutifully carried his lunch to Ellen.

Richard, cheerily honking his horn as he pulled in the driveway, brought final arrivals. His old beige Chevy teemed with the flailing arms and excited faces of the kids we'd agreed to transport.

Gail, Rodney, Maria, Carlos and José spilled out the doors, carrying instant energy into the yard.

"Circle time!" I called, eager to get started.

"Circle time!" Dave echoed, his hand on Adam's shoulder.

Ellen brought Skipper, her footsteps paced to his lurching gait.

Bill crawled under the shrubbery by the cellar door. Knees drawn to his chest, Tim inched in deeper until his back was against the outside wall of the house. There was nowhere left to hide. Finally Bill appeared, leaves caught in his hair and Tim's hand firmly in his. Tim looked longingly back at the bushes.

Frankie's mother, in stiff new blue jeans and starched pink shirt, remained as she promised, but looked confused about whether to sit on the grass with everyone else, or go to her son, whose fingers alone were visible from behind the big tree he was clutching.

"Come over here, Frank!" she called plaintively, patting the ground to her right.

No response.

Grinning, Maria and Carlos raced across the grass to take his place. Carlos won, collapsing breathlessly in the spot Mrs. Cassone was saving for her son. "Why don't he want to come?" Carlos pointed toward the tree. The woman stared back at him coldly, while Maria snuggled up to her left shoulder.

"Sit here, girl!" Gail, in huge pink sunglasses, white T-shirt and bright pink shorts, called to Ellen. She draped her arm possessively around Ellen's shoulder. Gail stuck out her tongue at Skipper, who was crawling onto Ellen's lap.

"Welcome to Camp Hopewell!" I looked around at the circle of children, their brown, peach and coffee-colored faces, the dazzling shades of their summer clothes, the blue, brown, black and hazel eyes that met or avoided my own. "Anybody feel a little scared about coming here today?" I asked. No answer. Blank expressions.

"I know I did." I continued. "Okay, we're going to roll this tennis ball around our circle. When you get it, you tell your name and pass it on. Like this: my name is Eleanor." I directed the ball gently across the circle.

"L-L-Laura." She pushed it away.

"Gail!" She kept her arm around Ellen.

Diane bit her fingernails. She mouthed her name but no one could hear it.

Maria whispered hers and handed the ball to her brother.

"Carlos." He shivered as though suddenly cold.

"I'm José, the oldest of them two right there," he said, pointing. Carlos scowled and made a fist. Maria smiled adoringly at her older brother.

When the ball rolled toward Adam, his fingers flew in the rapid motions of someone signing for the deaf. His head jerked, his eyes darted wildly. "In the name of heaven," he screamed, bolting away, "don't you know? Pow! Zak!" Halfway across the yard he cowered and covered his head protectively. "Don't you know?" His voice was pleading.

"It's okay, Adam." I went to him, aware of gasps from the circle. "The ball won't hurt you. No one's going to hurt you here."

He let me lead him back, his soft aqua eyes frozen in fear. "Whatever we're up against," he muttered, "it's our duty to repel . . ."

"Glad you're with us again, Adam. I'm Bill, and I'll be playing this guitar." Bill strummed a chord, then rolled the ball across the circle.

Rodney flopped down on his stomach and stretched out to reach the ball with his fingertips. "Big Man's the name," he grinned. "Smooching's my game."

Gail and Maria giggled. Ellen looked at me dubiously.

"I wanna hear the name"—Rodney pitched the ball toward the tree—"of that invisible creep over there." The ball rolled past Frankie's protruding foot.

His mother stiffened, her cheeks growing scarlet.

Silence. No response from Frankie.

"Okay, I'll say it for him." Burrowing his head in his arms, Rodney affected a squeaky voice. "Squirrel's my name and hiding's my game."

"No, Rodney. This is a place for helping, not for teasing," I said. "Maybe we can all help Frankie to join us."

"Shut up, you crazy witch!" Frankie yelled, still hiding. "I don't need any help. You just shut up!"

The kids looked from the tree to me to his mother.

Her eyes brimmed with tears. Suddenly she stood up and stumbled toward her son.

"Please continue, everybody," I nodded to Dave. "I'll be right back."

"My name is David . . ." I heard him begin.

Frankie had slumped to a sitting position, his back against the tree.

His mother knelt in front of him, her arms out like a beggar.

I touched his shoulder. "Frankie, please come. You can sit beside your mother . . ."

"Shut up!" His kick just missed my shins. "Shut up, I told you before, you wicked crazy woman!"

"Come back, Mrs. Cassone," I said, turning toward the trembling woman. "Frankie's not ready to be in the group. Maybe he'll be ready later."

"Never!" he screamed, reaching out to grab his mother. "That's when I'll be ready—never! And don't you leave me, Ma! Don't go! Don't listen to that evil woman!"

"Please, son," she said, struggling to get up. He yanked her hair with a violent jerk, forcing her down to his side.

"Let go of me, Frankie, please." Pleading words, but her face and voice were strangely calm. "Please stop this, son. Please let me go—"

"You don't have to beg for your freedom," I said, angry now at both of them—the controlling boy and his submissive mother. "Frankie, you better learn that holding your mother against her will is illegal! A violation of—"

"Shut up!" he snarled. "Don't go! Stay with me, Ma. I'll die if you leave me! Don't listen to that wicked witch!"

He let go of her hair, but she didn't move away. Instead, she looked from me to Frank. "I better not leave my son today." Her voice was so low I had to strain to hear her. "I'll sit over here with him, at least for now." She bowed her head.

Frankie nodded, struggling to suppress a smile. I felt disturbed by her demeanor and by his reaction. But Frankie's tantrum was distracting to the kids in the circle. I decided any more attention right now to this frustrating pair risked everyone's well-being. "I hope you'll both get ready to join us—"

I walked away thinking of the descriptions I'd read in Frankie's folder. Violent behavior with the school nurse, even the principal, when they tried to separate him from his mother. Unreal, I thought, till I myself was a witness. What had happened in this family for the boy to imagine he'd die without his mother?

"My name is Richard," my older son was saying as I returned. "Some people," he said with a grin, "think that's too long. If you do, you can call me Rich."

"Oh, rich, huh? Well if you're rich, Big Man here is glad to know you," Rodney thrust out his hand. Laughing, Rich eased the ball toward Tim, who inched back, turning away.

It was Skipper who crawled into the circle to retrieve it. "Pee

budder," he said, tapping the ball on his helmet. "Pee budder."
Everybody laughed except Gail, who muttered, "Stupid." Skipper
giggled and did a kind of somersault roll to more smiles until Ellen
caught and held him.

Gail reached under Ellen's arm to pinch Skipper's bottom, and he
jumped.

"No, Gail." I caught her hand.

"Okay?" Bill's eyes checked mine. "Ready for the name song?" He
strummed several chords. "Who wants to be first to be sung to?"

"Me, huh, Bill? Please, okay?" Rodney waved his arms in Bill's
face. Bill began the simple song we'd chosen for learning names, re-
peating Rodney's and ending "How are you today?"

The music stopped. Rodney quickly replaced his grin with a
scowl. "Man, what a stupid song! How I am, huh? Well, hmmm . . ."
He made a thumbs-up gesture, looking around to command attention. "Big Man is all-ll-ll ri-i-i-right! In fact, Big Man"—he wriggled
his hips—"is DY-NO-MITE!"

"Okay!" Bill nodded. "Who do you choose?"

Rodney pointed to Diane.

"Rotten," she muttered. "That's how I am, rotten."

Ellen, said, "Super!" Adam sputtered "Pow!" and "Zak!" Tim
wouldn't answer. He turned his back to the group.

We had a hopping contest from the circle to the sign-up sheet
Richard had posted on the door of the barn. Maria and Laura wrote
their names under "Art with Ellen." Skipper clapped when Ellen invited him to join them.

When Rodney chose "Basketball with Rich and Dave," Gail
printed her name under Rodney's, each letter three inches tall.
Diane's writing was too faint to read. Adam shook his head in confu-
sion, and dropped the pencil Bill put in his hand.

Bill led Adam, Diane and Tim up the old wooden stairs to the second floor of the barn, where he and his friends had spent hours
creating a room in space once used for storing hay. An old brass oil
lamp still hung on a metal chain from the center beam under the
high peaked roof. Bill had tacked bright posters along the weathered
silver-gray barnsiding walls. One showed an acrobat balancing on a
beam with the message, "I can because I think I can."

Bill had found an old braided rug in the cellar and spread it over the wide-planked floor. On it he'd arranged two bridge tables with folding chairs, a record player, building sets and shelves of models, books and games. There were dolls in Ellen's old cradle, and a wooden dollhouse Bill had made.

He'd hammered boards across the dangerous opening that once served for pitching hay. It led, if one mistook it for a door, to a two-story drop to the blacktop surface below. He had left an opening the size of a little window.

Thinking Bill's group might be hard for him to manage alone, I followed them upstairs. He was showing them games they could play together.

Diane ignored Bill. She retreated to a corner with what looked like a diary she took from the big white pocketbook on her shoulder, and wrote or drew, turning away from the others.

Tim found Ann's old book on volcanos. He squatted in a corner opposite Diane, slowly turning pages. Adam lifted two small dolls from the cradle, and knotted the crib sheets around their shoulders. Clutching one caped figure in each of his hands, he guided their flights and frequent mid-air collisions. "Pow! Bamm! My mission is not foolproof, for you—splat!—you will be the fool!"

Bill, standing close to Adam, signaled with a nod and wave of his hand that I could go.

We'd planned to let this first activity period run about an hour, during which I would begin evaluating kids to see who needed to be tutored. But I decided to remain free instead, to move from group to group on this first morning.

I picked up the wicker basket full of the children's lunches and carried it from the garage up the steep wooden stairway to our kitchen. By rearranging Richard's supply of soft drinks and Ellen's cartons of yogurt I jammed all the metal lunch boxes and brown paper bags into the refrigerator.

From the kitchen window I could look out on Frankie and his mother, both sitting with their backs against the tree now. Her eyes were closed and he was watching her warily, his hand on her arm.

Further down the yard, Gail's arms flailed as she tried to keep José and Carlos from getting the basketball from Rodney. She leapt joyfully when Rodney sank the ball into the net, then frowned when he slapped hands with Rich and Dave but not with her.

Ellen had left the sliding barn door open. I could see Laura and Maria, draped in Richie's old shirts, painting on opposites sides of the easel.

Skipper seemed to be crayoning on the table. I couldn't see any paper. Ellen was already taping someone's picture on the wall.

Surveying the panorama, the sparkling pool, the balmy cloudless day, my own and other people's kids enjoying our back yard, I knew with a deep satisfaction that this was what I'd hoped for. Camp Hopewell had truly begun.

The rest of the morning, Ellie's group painted, Richie's played ball, the children with Bill remained isolated from one another, but involved.

At eleven I took a group to the kitchen to make dessert for lunch—a chance to measure, follow directions and produce a treat for everyone's pleasure.

Gail had to tour the whole downstairs before she was ready to help. "I could tell you was married, Eleanor," she said, bouncing on the living room couch. "Married ladies always have sofas."

Laura and Maria sifted flour, their chatter about their teachers punctuated by Adam's Bamms! and Kowbooms!

Adam broke the first egg with precision. "Add two," I told him and left to set the oven. When I returned twelve egg yolks topped the chocolate batter and Adam was bombing them all with the jagged shells. "Splat—k-k-pow! So far doom's been calling the signals. Boof!"

"Why ya' ain't gonna hit him?" Gail demanded.

"Is that what happened to you, Gail?" I asked her.

At lunch time, I helped the kids take turns using the outdoor toilet while Richard passed out paper towels at the faucet-hose he and Bill had rigged for washing hands. José and Dave carried the basket of lunches and two pitchers of lemonade to a shady spot near the pool. Ellen spread out blankets.

Little groups formed quickly. Skipper and Gail cuddled close to Ellen. Bill compared sandwiches with Adam. Rich and the older boys talked about their ball game. The quieter children, Tim and Diane, sat closest to me.

Listening to the babble of voices I thought how right it felt, to be with this group of children. Then Laura began to whimper.

"My lunch! Ooooh, my lunch!" She rubbed her eyes. "Somebody musta stole it!" She flattened herself on the grass face down, arms and legs thrashing, and began to wail. "Somebody stole my lunch!" The cries grew louder.

"Oh stolen, huh?" Rodney leapt to his feet. Hands on his hips he towered over Laura's writhing body. "Watch it, girl! Anyone call the Big Man a thief, that person be askin' for plenty of grief!"

"I didn't hear Laura accuse you, Rodney—"

"You keep outta this, Eleanor! I oughta know when I been accused!"

Laura screamed even louder. She kicked faster and harder. Bill went off to look for her lunch.

"Anyone else think Laura accused Rodney?" I asked.

"I didn't," Richard answered.

"Not me," Dave shook his head.

But Rodney was still angry. "Call me names again, girl," he said through clenched teeth, "and I might go to jail with all them losers, but you'll be holdin' ice cubes on your bruises—"

"Oooh, he hates me! He hates me!" Laura beat the grass with her fists.

"K-k-pow! Bamm!" Adam, who looked bereft with Bill gone, aimed an imaginary weapon at Laura. "Only my paralyzing ray will strip that she-devil of her power! Kaablam!"

"Oh no!" Rodney groaned. "You keep outta this, Batman—"

"Rodney, sit down," I insisted. "Leave Laura alone."

He did but kept his eyes on the girl while he bit into his sandwich. "Mmm, good! Sure glad I got MY lunch!"

"Ch—ch—choke on it!" Laura raised her head. Her eyes were tearless.

Maria looked on with compassion. Kneeling next to Laura she held out her own snack. "You want some chater chips?"

Laura punched the bag. Potato chips cascaded over the lawn. Rodney and Gail scooped up more than they could stuff in their mouths. Maria looked stunned.

"Laura, how could you?" Ellen asked, "when Maria was being so nice—"

"Who does she think she is?" José seethed, "doin' that to my sister?" He leapt up with both fists clenched.

"No, José!" I cuaght his arm, and Bill returned waving Laura's lunch.

"It was wrapped up in your towel." He stooped to place it by her hand. "Okay now?" Bill patted her shoulder. "Ready to eat?"

I saw a fleeting smile replaced by a very unhappy face by the time Laura sat up. Ellen caught it too. Her eyes met mine.

While I was distracted, Frankie's mother had headed toward the tree with his lunch, even though I had told them both if he wanted to eat he'd have to come and get it.

"No, Mrs. Cassone," I called. "I don't want you to do that!"

She returned with Frankie's lunch but glared at me through narrowed eyes. "He has to eat."

"This is where we eat," I replied.

I walked to the tree and squatted by his side. "Lunch time, Frank. We'd like you to join us."

"Shut up! Shut up!" He plugged his ears with his fingers. His mother smiled.

Although Frankie stayed away, lunch proceeded pleasantly. Staff and kids began swapping jokes and riddles.

"Why did the man put the clock on the roof?" Gail shouted, when Ellen suddenly gagged.

"Oh help!" She ran to the toilet, her hand clapped over her mouth.

She'd been offering Skipper a sip of lemonade. He threw it up with some food, and the mess was dribbling down his chin.

"Ugh! Puke!" Diane and Gail scampered away. Skipper looked puzzled by their reactions, as though vomiting was a commonplace occurrence.

Wiping his face, I looked at Skipper's lunch box for another napkin and found the bib his mother had packed. Suddenly I remembered her talk about his immature digestive system.

"Please, Mom," Ellen said, taking me aside when she returned, "keep Skipper away from me—from now on." Her hand on my arm was shaky, her face drained of its color. "I just can't handle anything like that."

We must have been talking when Mrs. Cassone took his lunch to Frankie. I didn't realize he had eaten till the breeze caught an empty plastic wrapper, carrying it from the tree across the lawn.

"Mrs. Cassone," I said, but she wouldn't look in my eyes. "We've got to work together if we're going to help your son."

After lunch, I put on my old blue bathing suit and stood in waist-high water, helping Dave assess each child's ability to swim. Tim clung to the railing of the pool stairs, now and then immersing his toes. José and Carlos, who'd eyed the pool so longingly before, huddled together on the terrace, staring at the water. Adam had stretched out on the Styrofoam surfboard, his arms behind his head like a sun worshipper on a beach towel. Richard and I smiled at one another as we watched him float in lazy circles while Maria and Gail churned up the water with their practice kicks.

The afternoon went quickly. It was a beautiful cloudless day. Seventy-five degrees. Not too hot for activities. Warm enough for children to dry quickly after the swim, in preparation for an all-camp game of baseball.

Laura was so surprised when she swung the bat and it hit the ball that she forgot to run. Her whole team screamed frantically. Tim, playing outfield, had bent to investigate an ant hill and the ball rolled between his legs, allowing Laura to hop to first base.

Adam bunted. "Outside force propels overgrown splinter!" he called as he ran. Unfortunately he remained on first when José got there, having hit a grounder. Two outs. But Laura made it to third.

Skipper was up. Richard squatted behind him, his hands on the bat. Together they hit what could have been a double. Richie trotted Skipper along the base line.

A little cheer made me look up the hill. Skipper's mother was peering over the fence, smiling.

Laura should have scored the winning run. But she was picking daisies. Hers was the final out.

José stormed off the field, fuming about women. Laura blushed and giggled.

Skipper's grin didn't fade even when Gail tapped the dome of his helmet, "Dum—dum. You lost the game. What's so funny about that?"

"Closing circle!" I called.

Don't forget lunch boxes!" Ellen called, carrying the wicker basket from the garage.

"Towels and swimsuits too!" Dave added.

Our first closing circle. I looked around the ring of faces, everyone's grimy, including the staff's. Gone the gleaming pastel shorts and tops I'd seen this morning. Clothes were covered with dirt and grass stains. My own hair felt plastered against my neck. Mental note: swimming should be last activity before our closing circle.

"What did you like best today?" I asked.

"Swimming!" "Baseball!" "Painting!"

While they called responses, somehow our old Labrador retriever Millie let herself out of the house and delighted the children by parading around inside the circle, nuzzling one after another in her insatiable quest for affection.

"Here, Camp Dog!" Rodney pulled on Millie's tail. "Big Man's the name. Dog-catchin's the game—"

"Here, Camp Dog. Camp Dog, come to me!" the children snapped their fingers for Millie's attention.

With a groan, the old dog finally settled between Richard and Tim, who curled up beside her, stroking her back while Bill taught a camp song to the tune of "I've Been Working on the Railroad."

"We're the kids from old Camp Hopewell . . ."

Rodney waved his arms like a conductor. Behind him Carlos whispered to his younger brother. José stuck out his tongue at Rodney's backside. Maria clung to Ellen until Gail pushed her.

Skipper clapped to Billy's rhythm. Frankie peeked from behind his tree. The counselors were the only ones who sang the camp song.

> . . . We like to laugh and play
> We're the kids from old Camp Hopewell
> Making friends the Hopewell way . . .

Dave had to rush to keep his private appointments, but before he left he came to me with a boyish grin and shook my hand. "Congratulations! I think it's my favorite camp!"

When Skipper's mother led him away, her face was beaming.

Frankie dashed for the car when his mother got the motor running. Adam bounded toward his aunt. "Though bereft of my power," he called, leaping across the lawn, "I do not crawl or whimper! For I am still the Silver Surfer!"

Richard had trouble gathering up his car pool to drive them back to the community center. Rodney started a basketball game with Carlos and José. Gail insisted on helping Ellen collect the crayons. Maria swept out the barn. When they finally drove away, the children called back, "Goodbye! See ya tomorrow!" long after the car was out of sight.

Finally, only Diane was left. No one answered at her home. Bill sat with her till her mother's boyfriend brought his Porsche to a screeching halt by the gate. "Hurry up!" the man commanded. No apology for being late.

After the car squealed down the road I spotted something under the bush where Tim had hidden. With the help of a rake I retrieved an astronomy book of Bill's, and brought it to him.

Stretched out on the lawn, he accepted the book with a nod, squinted at me steadily and chewed on a long blade of grass. "So this is what it's going to be like? Like this, all summer long?" Bill asked. "Did it ever occur to you we could have had a camp for *normal* kids?" He was, I thought, trying to sound exasperated. But he looked intrigued and pleased.

It was still as warm and bright as midday when I left home two hours later for my six o'clock appointment at the clinic.

Backing out of the driveway, I could hear Richie playing his drums in the basement to the background of a recording of the Beatles singing "A Hard Day's Night."

The kids had made it very clear that I wasn't to concern myself with fixing their meals. And yet, because it was I who was leaving them, I felt a nagging guilt about not even being in the house at supper time. Irrational, I knew. A lingering desire to be needed, I told myself, heading on to the Post Road.

7

When Laura's mother dropped her off on Tuesday morning the girl collapsed face down on the ground. At first I thought she had tripped and fallen. Then she looked up in midscream to see if her mother was watching. Laura and I felt the wake of pebbles and dirt spin in our direction as her mother's car sped away.

"B-b-bitch!" Laura sobbed but her eyes were tearless. "I told her I wanted mustard on my sandwich, b-b-but she only gave me butter—"

"So your mother didn't give you what you wanted . . ." I helped her up.

Frankie wouldn't leave the car, so his mother gave up coaxing him and took her paperback book to a webbed lounge chair near the pool. Then he darted from the back seat to hide behind the same tree as he had the day before. Shade would be a welcome relief. It was a humid 80° and climbing.

Richard drove in with Gail, Rodney and the Hernandez children, all calling out, flailing arms and towels. I told them to put away their lunches quickly and come to opening circle. Dave, Bill and Ellen were already sitting with the other children.

Carlos and José made a space for me between them. Skipper climbed into my lap as Bill began the opening song. Across the lawn, Frankie sank down, his back against the tree, and plugged his fingers into his ears. Mostly it was the counselors who sang, with an occasional warble from Gail, or a deep bass contribution from Rodney.

"Hi, Adam; Hi, Adam. How are you today?" Adam cocked his head. He studied Bill's face, then his hands on the strings of the guitar, but he didn't answer the question we all sang to him.

Rodney, next to Adam, jumped up instead. "Me? You askin' me?" He flashed a dazzling smile. "Well, the Big Man is all right! In fact the Big Man is more than"—he swiveled his hips then rocked on them pointing both thumbs toward the sky—"more than DY-NO-MITE!"

"All-ll ri-i-ight!" Gail clapped admiringly, and Maria and Laura joined in the applause for Rodney. Gail made an ugly face at the girls, ending their enthusiastic reaction.

When Bill asked Tim how he was, he muttered, "Not very good" but refused to say any more. He sat with his arms locked around Millie, the dog.

"This morning"—again I held out the ball—"when this ball comes to you it's your turn to tell which child you are in your family, whether you have brothers and sisters or you're the only one, and how you feel about that. Like this—I'll begin. I'm Eleanor. I have an older sister Marie and a younger sister Claire. I was the second child. My brother John is the youngest. I used to think it was better to be oldest or the youngest than being in the middle—"

"I'll never answer that dumb question!" Rodney exploded, " 'cause being the youngest kid stinks—that's why!"

"I agree with that"—Laura lifted her head from Ellen's shoulder—"I'm not tellin' either."

"I don't mind being youngest." Ellen looked from Rodney to Laura. "Richard and Bill here are both my older brothers."

"Hey," Rodney leaned past Laura to elbow Richard in the stomach. "That girl really your sister?" he pointed to Ellen. "Man, I be thinkin' maybe she was your honey. Man, ain't you got no honey?"

"Think I'd tell you?" Richie laughed.

"Well now," Rodney rose and strutted, hands in the rear pockets of his jeans, to stand in front of Ellen, "you got a main man, girl? Maybe me, the Big Man, could have a whirl. Huh? What you think?"

Ellen laughed and glanced at me.

Gail was scowling. "That girl don't look like no sister to me." She glared at Ellen through narrowed eyes from across the circle. "I bet," she muttered, "she's nothin' but a—a prostitute." She said it softly but Rodney heard.

"What?" He yanked Gail to her feet by a handful of her yellow sweat shirt. "What d'you say about my girl friend?"

Gail looked stunned. Her jealousy of Rodney's attention to Ellen had backfired. Now he was in a rage at her. She didn't even raise her hands in self-defense. He pulled her up and then pushed her down. She landed on the broad bottom of her bright pink shorts, her legs in the air. Laura and Maria giggled.

Richard caught Rodney. "You got no permission to lay your hands on me!" the Big Man railed. "Let go! I'm gonna beat her ass!"

Frankie must have heard his mother's gasp. He peeked out at her with a worried look. Tim hid his face in Millie's fluffy fur. Around the circle the children sat frozen in attitudes of fear or tension.

"Listen, Mr. Big Man," Gail was embarrassed. She got up slowly, brushing dirt from her bottom, but her head was bowed, her eyes remained lowered. "Anybody beat my butt it won't be you, 'cause I whipped much bigger dudes than you where I come from." Although the words were tough, the delivery was unconvincing.

"What you want, girl?" Rodney, still held by Richard, surveyed Gail's chunky body with a sneer. "A medal or a chest to pin it on?"

"I must alert my duplicate"—Adam shadowboxed the air—"to freeze and to burn, to parch and to flood. K-k-pow!"

"Hey, honky." Rodney turned away from Gail to look over his shoulder at Adam, sitting in the circle. "Hey honky, you crazy!" Rodney tapped his temple in a derogatory way, pleased when some of the children laughed.

"Whatever we're up against," Adam said, dodging imaginary blows, "it's our duty to repel."

Rodney, diverted to this new target, shucked free of Richie's arm and ambled over to Adam and looked down at him in disgust. Adam covered his head with his arms and began to whimper. Rodney watched a moment before his face began to soften. He knelt before the cowering boy and touched his hand to Adam's knee.

"Really, honky." Rodney's voice was tender. "Listen, I'm sorry if I have to be the one to tell you, but you really is a little crazy."

• • •

The rest of the morning we tried to keep Gail and Rodney apart. I sat on the grass with Gail who muttered face-saving descriptions of countless fights at school she'd easily won. She'd even beaten up six boys. She paused to look longingly at Rodney.

I brought her to Ellie, whose charges were painting a mural on a six-foot-long sheet of newsprint. I wanted time with Tim, who'd retreated to the bushes when Billy gathered a group for a "rock-collecting expedition," resisting my suggestion that he join the explorers.

"I don't need to go with them. I've already made a friend." Tim backed further into his cavern of leaves, and I felt a little foolish to be kneeling on the grass, addressing a shaking shrub. "This dog is my friend." He kissed Millie's nose. "I like her better than all the people here or anywhere else on earth. . . ."

Finally Tim agreed to go with Billy, provided he could take paper and pen ". . . for making notes. I'm either going to be a geologist or a paleontologist, you know." His knuckles were white with tension as he clutched the pad of paper to his scrawny chest, as if preparing for battle.

Slumped against the tree, his eyes shut, Frankie only mumbled "Shut up" when I tried to talk to him. He smashed the model I brought for him to make. "That'll cost you a dollar," I said.

"I'll never pay, you crazy woman!"

It was such a sweltering day that I agreed with Dave's idea to interrupt activities for an earlier-than-scheduled all-camp swim, hoping it would cool us all off. But my visions of peace were short-lived.

Screams erupted in the garage where the boys were changing. In spite of Richard's presence, Adam had grabbed José's genitals as he put on his swim trunks. "Fag!" José stormed out, incensed, his towel whipping behind him like a flag. "Keep that weirdo freak away from me or I'll kill the little fag!"

Later, from his float in the water, Adam reached out wordlessly to pinch the bodies of the girls.

"Pervert! Weirdo pervert!" Gail screamed, scrambling up the metal ladder.

"Weirdo pervert!" Maria echoed seconds later.

Dave pulled Adam out of the pool and sat beside him in a chair for a talk. But Adam only looked around him, bewildered.

"What the devil's going on here?" He examined his hands, holding them close to his eyes. "There's proof that doom is nearing! The Silver Surfer is condemned to earth . . ."

"Someone oughtta ground that spaceship!" Gail complained.

"My daddy's gonna get you, boy!" Maria yelled.

At noon Bill stood beside me to help pass out the lunches. "Adam obviously isn't ready—or trustworthy—to do much with the other kids," he said. "I'd be glad to spend more time with him alone. Maybe we could look at my old super-hero comics, if you don't think that would reinforce his problem."

I was touched by the caring I heard in Billy's voice. For all his grown-up restraint, he could still identify with a fearful boy who looked to super-heroes for strength and protection.

It was, I said, a hopeful plan, to try reaching Adam by starting where his fantasies focused. Maybe from that beginning Billy could introduce other magazines and books more geared to reality than comics. But I warned Bill not to get his hopes too high.

While the other children swam, played baseball or sculpted with clay, Adam spent the period after lunch with Bill, reading aloud the stylized language of the comic-book tales. "His bestial strength will be rendered powerless by the anti-gravity field in which I have him entangled. If this deadly foe be too powerful an evil we must increase our strength to overcome the intruders."

The next day Bill was busy with other children, and Adam brought the super-hero comic books to me. I was at the picnic table, just finishing a phonics lesson with Maria.

"Okay, I'd be glad to read with you." I took the magazines he offered. "Come sit beside me." I patted the redwood bench.

Adam rested his head against my shoulder, the same position he had taken with Bill. "In all the galaxy," he read with melodramatic expression, "none match the helplessness of those who inhabit tortured earth!"

"You read hard words," I told him. "Good for you!"

At first I thought it was a friendly gesture, Adam stroking my hair, my shoulder. But then he slipped his hand inside my T-shirt and squeezed the cup of my bra.

Stunned, I spoke brusquely. "Adam! Keep your hands to yourself!"

"I can dally with you no longer," he muttered, unzipping his pants to fondle himself.

"No, Adam. Pull up your zipper." I hadn't expected his hand on me, but I wasn't surprised at his touching himself. Other children got satisfaction from relationships and achievement. Adam had neither and sought comfort from his body. His reaching for other children was a greater concern. Although I explained that it wasn't allowed, the issue was really his lack of control, evident in all areas.

I alerted Bill and Dave to keep an eye on Adam, especially in the water or when children were changing their clothes. But Adam was hard to watch. When Bill and I weren't free to be with him, he'd wander away from groups to pace around the swimming pool or up and down the driveway flashing signals with his fingers and talking to himself. Dave, Richard and Ellen all tried to involve him, but Adam needed individual help.

In spite of the problems, or perhaps because of the challenge they presented, I loved getting up in the morning, waiting for the kids to arrive. And I felt proud of my own kids—the activities and games they planned, the way they handled their responsibilities.

For my part, I delighted in the chance to teach again. Before I went back for my master's degree, I had spent eight years as a teacher, and I had missed some satisfactions of the "ordinary" classroom.

It was fun to reassemble my teaching materials at the picnic table, a site which afforded me a panoramic view of the yard. A sturdy old typewriter for the kids to use, word games, a wide assortment of books, paper and pens for them to make books of their own—my favorite way to help children with reading.

The stories they wrote, the pictures they drew, let me understand each child a little better. Gail listed the kids she'd played with when she lived in the project with her mother.

"Let's see. Girls: Rhonda, Sharon, Nettie . . . I wonder if they'll remember me when I go home."

Gail refused to consider the possibility that she might never return. "You'll see, Eleanor. You'll see. My mother gonna tell that judge she come to get me."

Her drawings dealt with the feelings children experience when they have been removed from home to live with strangers. She drew the building her family lived in. "We was 15A . . ." Stick figures of her brothers and sisters. "Ralph, he useta hit my mother if she be drinkin'. Ina Claire, she sleep in my bed. This be the baby. I love him best. He didn't go to no foster home. He hadda go to a hospital . . ."

Gail drew her foster family, but then ripped up the paper.

"I won't be seein' them no more. Soon as my mother get all her checks she buyin' a house for all us kids to live in. She probably be goin' up and down the street right now. Just lookin' . . ."

A little picture on the inside cover showed a house with flowers in the garden and smoke curls wafting from the chimney. On the lawn in front of the door, Gail carefully printed a sign: "House for Sale, 1¢."

Biting her lip, she stared at the picture a long long time before she slammed the book shut.

The other children's books were equally revealing. Rodney wrote about motorcycle races—speeding, breaking away. As he drew he talked about his mother. "I dunno what that woman want. I guess she want me under a desk like a boss man. But I want my future more like drivin' a racer."

The sketches Rodney drew on the inside cover expressed interests less innocent than his fascination with motorcycles: an erect penis and a marijuana cigarette.

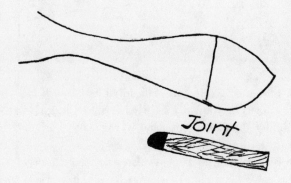

Adam's book had no words. Just pictures of monsters he called "Frankinmom and Frankindog" and close-ups of their teeth.

What a frightening world this child inhabited.

Tim didn't need or want my help with his writing. He took his book back under the azalea bush and would have worked there all day long if I'd let him.

For each picture that he drew he also wrote an extensive legend. The first one, which he read to me, began: "The male tyrannosaurus rex is fighting with the female brontosaurus. This scares the baby pterodactyl in the middle, but he's too afraid to fly away . . ."

Laura, who had serious academic problems, dictated stories about issues that kept her too preoccupied to learn. It was better use of her time than sounding out new words. But she did draw a picture for me of a mother deer kicking its baby.

"Why did the mother do that?" I asked, seeing her drawing.

"It's what the baby gets. For crying all the time."

"But babies have to cry—"

"Uh-uh. This one was bad. Now she'll hafta walk crooked."

"Laura," I said, brushing a strand of hair from her almond brown eyes, "do you think that's what happened to you?"

"Uh-uh. My mother didn't do that. But every time she changed my diapers, she useta twist my leg in—that's how come I'm a cripple."

"No, Laura. Your leg turned in when you were born."

"It didn't! It didn't! My mother did it—because I useta cry—"

I was still working with Laura when Tim returned to the picnic table for scraps of wallpaper to make a cover for his book, "Life Before Recorded History."

"Sit at the table," I urged him, before he went back to the bushes. I hoped he and Laura would talk to each other. They worked in total silence for over five minutes.

"I don't have much friends." Laura finally ventured.

Tim watched thoughtfully while she scribbled grass on her drawing. "Well," he said slowly, "I really don't have any friends myself, although I don't know why that should be."

"Neither do I," Laura mused. "Nobody never wants to play with me."

"No one in my entire neighborhood plays with me either," Tim paused to study the cover he was making. "And I can't understand it, since I don't have bad legs like you."

Laura shoved her book off the table and hobbled away, whimpering.

"Now why did she go?" Tim watched with a puzzled expression.

"O-o-o-oh!" the girl wailed. "Everybody hates me!" She flung herself to the ground. Tim remained at the picnic table, troubled but utterly unable to understand her. "I was only being honest!"

Bill's and Richard's groups gathered for closing circle. By now the kids were used to seeing Laura thrashing and wailing. They simply stepped over her body. Each of the Puerto Rican children always said "Excuse me."

But Gail, who was leaving the barn with Ellen, called across the yard to Laura. "Course we hate you, girl! And you deserve it! You wanna know why? Why everybody hate you?"

" 'C-c-cause"—Laura looked up and sniffled—"it's 'cause I'm crippled—"

"Right!" Gail kept walking toward Laura as she yelled. "But it ain't because of your leg. You ain't comin' here on accounta your leg. You, girl, you is crippled in the head! That's why you're comin' to this nut camp!"

There was a heavy silence. Rodney, who was waiting for closing circle, stared uncharacteristically into space. Diane, sitting near him, began to rock and hold her stomach. Carlos and José exchanged glances, then shook their fists at Gail.

Adam paced the driveway, banging his open palm against his forehead. "No place to hide! No place to give us shelter!"

"What do you mean by a nut camp?" I called to Gail. I could feel Tim's body trembling on the bench beside me. He and others who came to us from special classes must have suffered these ugly labels. We had to deal with it now.

Even Adam paused to watch Gail saunter toward me, squinting in the sunlight. "Huh! You're the one who started this, Eleanor. You oughtta know what's a nut camp. A place for crazy kids who can't do nothin' right—"

"Then you're wrong, Gail," I looked her straight in the eye. "I wouldn't run a nut camp. I work with kids I've got a lot of hope for. Gutsy kids who'll face up to their problems."

Diane sat up straighter. Rodney nodded. "Right on, sister."

8

That night driving to our first parents' meeting I felt nervous. Group work with adults was new territory for me. What if no one came? And what if they did?

Some of them were already in the waiting room when I arrived, and Dave was adding folding wooden chairs to the motley assortment he'd arranged in a circle in his sparsely furnished office.

The parents filed in awkwardly—Mrs. Hernandez, looking due to have her baby any moment; Diane's and Rodney's mothers, Laura's, Tim's and Skipper's parents, Adam's aunt and uncle, Gail's foster parents, Frankie's father but not his mother.

No smiles or greetings. Silently, self-consciously each found a place to sit.

Needing some structure myself, I suggested we introduce ourselves by taking something from our wallets or pockets that might help others know us.

"I'm Eleanor. This is a picture of my children. Here's the key to my office, and the pad of paper I carry to make notes for my writing . . ."

Shyly, Mrs. Hernandez showed her rosary beads, Diane's mother proudly displayed a new semi-precious ring from "a wonderful friend," Rodney's mother the keys to the offices she cleaned, Laura's parents a picture of their daughter when she was born—"before we realized her problem. . . ."

Gail's foster mother dug in her purse for a letter from the Division of Protective Service stating that the hearing for termination of Gail's biological mother's parental rights would come up in July. A more definite date would follow.

"My husband and I," the articulate black woman nodded toward the bearded gentle-eyed man beside her, "are hoping to adopt Gail. This hearing will be the first step. Our own three sons are grown and we—we lost our only daughter years ago. . . . Her name was Effie."

"I didn't know that, Mrs. Bennett." I was stunned that this information was nowhere on the record of Gail's foster placement. Nor had it been mentioned in our meetings at the clinic.

"We try not to talk about it." The woman closed her eyes. "She died of leukemia. She was only nine."

Her husband showed a faded photograph of their daughter, in a bathing suit, holding a pail and shovel. A thin little girl, standing on a sandy beach, grinning into the camera.

The protectively blank faces the adults presented walking in softened as the picture passed around. But for me it set off a kind of warning. If the Bennetts wanted Gail to replace their missing daughter, her adoption could be a disaster unless they'd really worked through their mourning. And the fact that they had never mentioned losing a child before made me wary. There was special work to be done with this family.

Mr. Bennett carefully slid the photo back in his wallet.

Frankie's father, beside him, quickly altered the mood. "Here's something that tells about me." He waved a twenty-dollar bill. "Here's what I'd spend if I could go out with my wife—the way we used to—before the kid ran the household. We loved to go to different restaurants for dinner. Now he won't let her out of the house.

"Would you believe we'll have to take turns at these meetings, and the kid's going to pitch a fit when I'm the one who stays home. Come to think of it," he drew another bill from his pigskin wallet, "I'm going to make it forty dollars! Forty dollars if my wife and I could spend an evening without the kid ending up in our bedroom." .

"Your kid in your bedroom?" Tim's father grimaced. "What do you do about sex?"

"Sex? What's sex?" Frankie's father drew on his pipe. "I can hardly remember."

The burst of self-conscious laughter dissolved reserve. Suddenly everyone had something to say.

Laura's mother, who'd been staring at her daughter's picture, spoke with a soft intensity that refocused the group's attention. "Here's my baby. She's going to the hospital in a week or so. It makes me feel so guilty—that my child will have to suffer."

Skipper's mother nodded sympathetically.

"It's Laura's third operation." Her mother looked beseechingly around the circle. "What's made it so much worse for me is Laura— Laura telling anyone who'll listen that I'm the one who hurt her. She's been told it happened before she was born but she likes to say I used to twist her leg when she was a baby. It's so upsetting to me."

"We don't know if Adam was born with his problem, or got that way because of his mother." Adam's uncle, a balding, ruddy-faced man about fifty, toyed with the visor of his painter's cap. "Maybe things woulda worked out better for the kid if we took him early on. But we only get to keep him when his mother—the wife's kid sister—gets carted off to the funny farm, over there at Fairview Hills. This time they picked her up walkin' naked right through the center of town. Yup," he nodded soberly to Tim's father's incredulous guffaw.

"See, I believe it's 'cause she took that dope—and smoked that mary-whana. Ran away from home when her mother died, right off to one of them, ah, communes—"

"We wanted to help my sister," Adam's aunt broke in, picking at her nails. "We even drove to the mountains, in western Massachusetts, to try to bring her home. There she was, only seventeen, with five strange-looking people in a log cabin with a dirt floor, barefoot, skirt hanging down to her ankles. I begged her to leave. But she was about to—to have a baby."

"Santa Maria." Mrs. Hernandez stroked her enormous stomach. Her eyes filled with tears.

"Wanted to have it in the cabin, without no doctor—" Again Adam's uncle took over the telling of the story. "So that's how the kid was born. An' we didn't even see him till she cracked up two

"My son could never be a salesman." Tim's father had come to the seven-thirty meeting straight from work, remarkably handsome in a light summer suit as vibrantly blue as his eyes. "I meet people all day long while my son spends his life avoiding contact. I'm out there beating the bushes, so to speak. Tim only wants to hide in them."

Frankie's father, a squat, dark-haired man, twisted his thin waxy moustache. "This is my eighth year on the faculty at Bridgeton," he said, "teaching accounting to business majors while my own son can't do simple math and never goes to school. Now how do you figure that?" He drew on his pipe.

Frankie would never be an accountant like his father. Adam could never earn a living as a carpenter like his uncle. Impossible dreams. Unreachable goals. Heavy burdens for the children. Maria's mother hesitantly shared her hopes for the girl to become a nun and at least one son to join the priesthood. "Only pray to God, I ask to my children, but each one, each one of them say to me, 'No, mama, no more, it makes our knees too sore . . .' "

The adults spoke in turn—politely—about their children in terms of their own expectations, until we got to Skipper's father. "My son"—the man nodded toward his wife and reached for her hand—"*our* son, may not live to be an adult. We don't worry about his schoolwork or how he'll earn a living. We just want to make his childhood as happy as possible."

"Me too," Laura's mother said softly. "But I never dreamed it would be so hard."

"Well!" Tim's father smacked his forehead in a mocking gesture. "That's what we get for forgetting!"

"I'm not sure what you mean—" I broke the awkward silence.

"Well, isn't that why all these kids were born?" Tim's father smirked. "Because one of us adults forgot to make a trip to the drugstore?"

Frankie's father chuckled, but Laura's mother was indignant. "No, that is not why all these children were born! You may speak for yourself, but not for me!"

Tim's mother's cheeks were flaming as Dave and I said goodnight to the group.

9

Friday. The last day of the first week of our camp. The morning news predicted rain—a contingency we hadn't yet planned for—but the sun was bright as the kids began to arrive, and stayed that way all morning.

By now everyone knew the routine. Right after opening circle the children chose their first activity—swimming, drama, sports or art. One at a time they worked with me at the picnic table. Otherwise they remained in groups.

At noon the sky suddenly darkened. Thunder rolled and the wind pitched in gusts across the lawn. We'd have to eat in the barn. Amid the flurry of reorganization I wondered what would happen with Frankie, when for the first time everyone, including his mother, left his line of vision. Would he finally be forced to join us?

Bill and Ellen directed children from toilet to wash-up to the barn. José helped Richard bring orange juice and paper cups from the house to the table Ellen used for art. Frankie's mother stayed outside pleading with him till the rain came—at first a drizzle, then a downpour—and she too ran for shelter.

I pulled the heavy sliding doors almost shut, leaving only enough space for the boy to enter.

The children were all excited about eating in the darkened room. They sat in random groupings on the wide-planked floor, giggling, telling riddles and jokes while the rain beat on the old shingled roof. José passed cups of orange juice around. Gail shared her "chater chips." Diane even accepted half of Richard's sandwich. Though her face flushed and she barely nibbled, she smiled each time he looked in her direction.

Only Laura was unhappy. She toppled to the floor, kicking and screaming about hating rain. When no one paid attention, she "found" her lunch in the carton Ellen used for scraps, snuggled close to Dave and ate.

"Why was Columbus a cheat?" Rodney yelled.

"I know! I know!" Billy jumped up like a kid. " 'Cause he double-crossed the ocean!" Everybody laughed.

It was still raining when we finished the cookies I'd made with Gail, Skipper, Adam and Diane. Bill reached for his guitar and began to play. Adam huddled by his side watching Bill's fingers as though it puzzled him to see motions that could create and change the musical sounds.

As everyone began singing "I've been workin' on the railroad, all the livelong day . . ." I saw a form flash past the door then return a few seconds later from the opposite direction. "Singin' fee fi fiddle-ee-i-ohhh! Fee fi . . ."

Frankie darted around the barn again, this time tapping on the windows. His mother, now flanked by Carlos and Maria, sang as though she didn't notice. Frankie appeared round and round again, at the side windows, the back of the barn, the gap at the door.

"Hey, Bill"—Gail lifted her head from Ellen's shoulder—"you know that song, He got the whole world in His hands?"

Even Tim, who was combing Millie's tail, joined in. Dave rocked with Laura. Diane grinned at Richie. Carlos and Maria cuddled Frankie's mother. Skipper crawled into my lap and clapped.

Then Gail's voice, strong and perfectly pitched, soared above the others, binding and thrilling us all.

> *He's got you an' me, brother, in His hands,*
> *He's got you an' me, sister, in His hands—*
> *He's got the whole world in His hands.*

Even Frankie, on about his tenth journey around the barn, paused briefly by the window.

Gail finished to an audience so enthralled it took a moment to clap.

"Gail," Bill shook his head, "how'd you learn to sing like that?"

"Sometimes"—she looked out the window—"my grandma useta come an' take us kids to church . . ."

"Let's sing to Camp Dog," Tim suggested from the corner of the room.

"He got Camp Dog Millie in His hands . . ." Gail rallied from her daydream to lead the group again, while Rodney waved his arms like a conductor. Frankie, completely drenched, still circled the barn, tapping harder now as he streaked by each window.

Rich, Ellen, Dave and I nodded to one another that we had seen and heard him, but his mother seemed to have forgotten all about her son. She was enjoying the attention from Carlos and Maria. "If you was my mom," I heard Carlos tell her, "you and me would be sooo tight." She slipped her arms around the children, who smiled contentedly.

Suddenly a rock burst through the window, spraying glass everywhere. Instant chaos. The children ran in all directions, screaming.

The rock rolled to a halt at Mrs. Cassone's feet. Then came several smaller stones, wet mud, tiny pebbles. Carlos and Maria jumped up, their eyes round with terror. Frankie's mother sat frozen, a motionless target.

Ellen, Dave and Bill dashed around checking the children. Richard ran outside after Frank. I picked up the jagged shards of glass. Incredibly, no one was injured.

"That's what you get, you crazy wicked traitor! You female Benedict Arnold! That's what you get!" Frankie peered through the broken window. "Sure you act like you're happy here! But tell them what you said last night while Dad was at their meeting! How much you hate this stinkin' camp and all these bossy people. Go ahead! Why don't you tell them?"

Richard clapped his hand on Frankie's shoulder and marched him into the barn.

His mother shook her head in denial, but her face grew flaming red.

Carlos and Maria backed closer to the children who'd gathered in the corner and Rich led Frankie toward me.

Adam broke from the group to throw his two-fingered hex sign. "If we must go," he said trembling, "we've got to take doom with us!" Then he made a slashing motion across his throat.

"Calm down." Bill took Adam's hand. "It'll be okay . . ."

Frankie spat at Adam. He glared at his mother, inhaled deeply, then broke away from Richard and tore around the room, kicking dents in a metal locker, ripping down drawings, smashing clay sculptures. He eluded Dave, me, Rich, Bill and Ellen long enough to grab all the brushes from the paint jars and streak a rainbow of colors along the walls.

By the time Dave and I finally caught him, his mother was struggling to stand. Richard put out his hand to help her.

"Sure, Rich, sure!" Frankie screamed, his face a vivid purple. "Be nice to HER! Never mind how mean you were to ME!" Frankie broke away from Dave and me to speed out the door—right over to his special tree. Ragged clouds still scudded by overhead, but the storm was over. The emerald grass was glistening, steaming, as the summer sun began to reabsorb the rain.

Billy slid the heavy barn doors open. One by one the sober children stepped outside, some protecting their eyes from the sudden brightness.

I walked over to Frankie, who was scrunched up like a ball, shaking and sobbing, and sat down beside him. I was instantly sorry, because the grass was very wet. He let me pat him but wouldn't raise his head. Still I felt hopeful about his letting me see his sadness. I felt angry at his mother. I believed she really had talked against the camp, and probably against the people at his school as well, covertly undermining efforts to help him, yet keeping her distance now when he really needed her near him.

"I like you, Frankie," I said softly. "I'd like to help you."

Then Rodney shouted, "Hey, everybody, will ya look at that!" He pointed above the barn.

Glowing arches of purple, green, yellow, orange-red spanned the sky. Even Frankie peeked at the shimmering rainbow.

I looked at Bill, whose arms were around Skipper and Adam; Gail and Maria, on the grass with Ellen, their heads on her lap; Rich, with

Diane's and Carlos' arms around his back; Rodney in front, his hands on his hips. All were silently watching the brilliant rainbow fade away until it disappeared.

Frankie whispered, but I only caught the end of his statement. ". . . no matter what they think, my mother said it. She hates this camp a lot. A whole lot more than I do."

10

How was your weekend?

—How was your stinkin' crummy weekend? Rodney mocked Bill's question. That's none of your business. 'Cause it sucked. That's how it was. It sucked.

—We just stayed in.

—We didn't do nothin' 'cept my tooth fell out and I put it under my pillow but nothin' didn't happen . . .

—The tooth fairy must be dead.

—Our father hit our mother . . .

—*Madre de dios!* He'd kill us if he knew you told!

—My mother says I'm gonna get my operation—Friday.

—In addition to reading about dinosaurs, I was studying spiders and other nauseating insects. Now, where oh where is dear little Camp Dog . . .

—Mr. Bennett caught me bein' good so he took me to McDonald's.

—K-K-Krack, k-pow!

—Pee budder.

—My stomach ached the whole time I was with my father. And I was counting on a movie, but he got tickets to a play instead. Next Saturday he promised me a makeup date, so we can do what *I* say. And he owes me fifteen dollars.

It was the most Diane had said since she came to camp.

"Fifteen dollars!" Rodney gasped.

"So what! I have to buy my own records and all my makeup with that."

The circle broke and Ellen's art group gathered. But she ran up to the house. I thought at first she'd forgotten something she needed for the children, but when she didn't return I left Skipper with Dave and found Ellen by the kitchen sink, blotting her eyes with a damp paper towel.

"It really got to me," she sniffled. "That kid, Diane. She's such a little brat! I—I can't stand hearing her complaints about her father. Especially—especially when it's so long since I've seen Dad."

My heart ached for Ellie but I didn't tell her. "Come on El, toughen up. It got to you because you let it. You don't have to let yourself get hurt—" I wanted to add more but either the wind or Ellen slammed the kitchen door.

I watched her from the window as she ran across the yard. What had made me so brusque? I'd been kinder to troubled clients than to my daughter. But I had never felt the burden of their pain. Ellen's was harder to deal with. Her tears aroused my guilt. And compassion. She mustn't be so sensitive and easily wounded—a battle I had fought with myself for years.

I'd explain this to her—later. For now the incident somehow strengthened my resolve to bring about a healthier distance between Frankie and his mother. But Mrs. Cassone seemed reluctant when I asked her to meet with Frank and me right away.

In spite of his mother's reluctance to talk, I felt a new ease with Frankie. He didn't back away or try to block his ears when I spoke. But when I got to the vital point that either he participate in activities or his mother would have to leave, he reverted to his old behavior.

"Shut up, you crazy fool!" He clapped his hands on his ears. "I'm never doin' nothin' with any of these wicked people!"

"Then that's your decision. Tomorrow"—I turned to his mother, who was kneeling beside him—"you'll have to go, right after opening circle. Just be sure you say goodbye to Frank."

"She'll never say goodbye to me, you nutty woman! She'll never leave me at this wicked place alone. Never! Will you mother! Will you!"

"I'll—I'll come back early, son." She swallowed.

"No! No!" He cradled his head in his arms. "Don't leave me with this crazy bitch! Don't do it to me, mother!"

Sliding closer, she rocked him in her arms, his head against her breast. Frankie's thumb found its way to his mouth.

The phone by my bed began to ring at a quarter to seven on Tuesday morning.

"I've been up all night with my son." The woman's voice was shaky.

"I know you're tired, but it's very important to bring him—"

"We can't," she said flatly. "He's been having palpitations and now his stomach's hurting—"

"Please, Mrs. Cassone, if Frankie doesn't come today those feelings will be worse the next time. We've got to help him overcome them."

But they never did show up, and although I was disappointed, the time I would have spent on Frankie was put to good use with Laura, who had three more days at camp before her operation.

She'd visited the hospital with her mother, even been shown the recovery room "where they said I'd wake up," but Laura wasn't sure that she would wake up.

Billy had found a crumpled paper on which she had written:

When Ellen asked if she'd like to take her weaving loom to the hospital, Laura answered ". . . no, just leave it in my will."

Instead of the graceful illustrations she'd drawn in her book of stories, Laura's pictures now showed primitive figures—"a mother" in a witch's hat, with a tiny father in the background.

"Do they have any kids?" I asked her.

Adam made nothing for Laura, but began to repeat a new fantasy game with Bill, dressing smaller dolls in capes of Kleenex. Mighty Man swooping in to rescue Super Girl from the hands of Dr. Doom.

I was thinking of Laura as I was getting dressed for my five o'clock appointment at the clinic. I wanted to leave early enough to stop at the Cassones'.

But Dr. Bialek's secretary called just as I was going out.

"We've got the mother of one of your campers here, sitting in the waiting room. She insists on seeing Dr. Bialek. Apparently she's got some complaint concerning you. He wants you here in twenty minutes."

I was certain that complainant would be Frankie's mother and wasn't even thinking of Diane until the receptionist directed me into the waiting room. "Mrs. Woodruff's fuming about waiting for you but Dr. Bialek refused to see her alone."

He sat behind the huge mahogany desk, assessing the woman appreciatively as she sauntered into his office, outdistancing me by several yards.

Legs crossed, she began to weep the moment she sat down.

"My husband wants to see Diane again next weekend . . ." The visits were intolerable but no one—she glared at me coldly—would help her to prevent them. She came with the hope that he'd be the one compassionate professional who'd deny her former husband's right to see his daughter.

"I read the records." Dr. Bialek tapped his thick manila folder. "All your previous therapists believe the man is doing everything he can to maintain an appropriate relationship with his daughter. You cannot expect me to take a one-sided position. But we'll gladly do our best to help you and your daughter in terms of your emotional needs."

Her voice was icy. "Obviously neither of you clearly understands the situation!"

The psychiatrist calmly wrote out names of three other doctors, then handed the list to the startled woman. "One of these people may understand it better than Mrs. Craig or I."

"You mean, I'm supposed to shop for a psychiatrist until I find one who agrees with me?"

"Or else," the doctor nodded, "one who agrees with me. Perhaps two opinions will help you change your mind."

Her eyes grew narrow. Her mouth drew tighter. Harsh lines from the corners of her lips to her nostrils. "You're angry with me, aren't you?"

"Oh no." He rose extending both hands. "Maybe twenty years ago I would have been. But not any longer. Twenty years ago I wanted all our clients to think I understood them. Now I'm content to settle for the satisfied nine out of ten."

As soon as I turned down the driveway, Richard switched on the floodlights and walked across the yard. "Your friend called, Ma. Ceil Black. She wants us to take a new kid in the camp. Tomorrow. An emergency, she says. His mother went to the hospital this afternoon. Mrs. Black had to pick him up, so she'll call you in the morning."

Her call woke me up on Wednesday morning at 6 A.M. Apologizing for the timing she said she hoped she wasn't pushing our friendship, presuming that I'd take the boy.

". . . the doctor says he saved his mother's life. He found her unconscious yesterday afternoon and picked up the phone to tell the operator he couldn't wake her. A suicide attempt.

"He insisted on riding in the ambulance and sat alone in the waiting room long after they pumped out her stomach and put her in the psychiatric unit. No one realized the boy was still there.

"Finally at ten o'clock last night one of the nurses found him sleeping behind a chair. The boy began to cry and asked her to call me. I used to work with him every week at his school.

"When I picked him up he insisted on going home so I left him at the project with an upstairs neighbor he calls Aunt Josephine. She's not related, but he's stayed with her before.

"El, I knew him as a troubled kid but now he really needs help. He shouldn't be alone now, and Josephine goes to work all day. I'll bring him early, if that's all right with you. His name is Nathaniel."

He was short for ten, barely up to my shoulder, but Nathaniel had instant appeal—intense, almond-shaped eyes like my son Bill's, a perfectly rounded head with tightly cropped shiny black hair, caramel colored skin, a serious, yet mobile face.

But I was caught by the dignity with which Nathaniel wore someone else's clothing.

The neck of his man-sized T-shirt was so big his shoulders were exposed, and the legs of the jeans were rolled into bulky cuffs, the crotch drooping close to his knees. He'd gathered the waist with a strand of clothesline long enough to wrap around him twice.

Nathaniel wouldn't look at me, or Bill or Ellen. His eyes fixed on the big glass jar he cradled in his elbow. The lid was dotted with puncture holes. Blades of bright green grass inside kept jumping. Then I spotted the shiny green snake.

"You could leave your jar on the porch," I suggested when greetings failed to elicit an answer.

"No way!" He had a surprisingly deep and gravelly voice. "Killer goes wherever I go."

"It's the only thing he brought from home." Ceil's eyes met mine.

"Then keep the lid on," Bill cautioned. "Our dog, Millie, sometimes catches snakes."

"Will Nathaniel need a bathing suit?" Ceil looked toward the pool.

He could borrow one from the drawerful of extras Ellen had collected for the children, but that was not the problem. His mother had to sign a permission slip before we could legally let him in the water. Nathaniel looked unhappy as we discussed the dilemma.

Finally, Ellen and Bill took him to the kitchen to make his lunch while Ceil and I had coffee on the porch and talked about Nathaniel. The boy would stay with Aunt Josephine until his mother got out of the hospital, perhaps anther week or more. Ceil herself would pick him up after camp this afternon. Then he could ride with Richard's car pool. "I feel a little guilty dropping him on you so suddenly, El . . ."

"It's okay." I grinned, thinking of how many kindnesses she'd done for me. "Really, I don't mind adding another kid. Next year we'll start with twenty or more—"

"Next year?" She smiled. "You're already planning."

"So what's a pilot program without a follow-up?" I hadn't even told myself how much I hoped the camp would continue—wherever I lived.

All during opening circle the children's eyes kept returning to Nathaniel. Rodney, like everyone else, looked anxiously at the stranger and the jar he held so tightly.

"How are you today, Rodney?"

"Okay." His eyes darted instantly toward the newcomer. Far from Rodney's usual "dy-no-mite!"

Nathaniel was the last to be sung to. None of the children rolled the ball in his direction to choose him. "Should we call you Nat or Nate or Nathaniel?" Bill smiled, strumming the guitar.

"Nathaniel!" Again I was started by his gravelly old-man's voice. "And my pet snake's name is Killer. An' I'm warnin' ya all that nobody better touch him, never! 'Cause just one command from me and Killer shoots his poison venom."

Few kids sang good morning to Nathaniel.

Morning discussion focused on pets, though the stories told had less than happy feelings.

"I used to have a pony," Diane said softly, rocking and massaging her stomach. "My father sold him without ever telling me, just before he went away . . ."

"I used to have my own dog," Tim said, stroking Millie, "but the kids in my neighborhood kept on kidnapping her every time I let her out."

"How'd they do that?" Rodney cocked his head.

"They always took her to their own yards to give her something to eat, and my mother got so sick and tired of trying to coax her back that she finally gave my dog away."

"I still have one duck." Laura kept her eyes on Millie-dog to tell her story. "But a mean dog got my other duck and ate his head off. And the duck I got still remembers his friend."

"When did all these sad things happen?" Bill asked.

"Four years ago," said Diane.

"Five for me," Tim murmured.

"Three years ago was when my duck got killed."

Sad events that happened long ago, being remembered by kids whose academic recall often failed them.

When we finished talking, the children scattered quickly. With a last glance at Nathaniel, Rodney ran to play ball with Richard. Ellen's group began a collage. Bill worked with Adam. Dave walked Skipper and a cluster of others toward the water.

"Have you seen dear little Millie?" Tim was looking under the azalea bush when I stopped him.

"No, Tim, but if you put on your swim trunks, Dave will teach you to float—"

"No, Eleanor, I have to find the dog. Millie! Millie! Where oh where is dear little Millie?" He wrung his hands.

I'd decided not to try to force Tim. Nor would I stay with him. Tim liked drawing off adults to get individual attention. But he got too much of that at home.

Instead, I chose to be with Nathaniel. I'd watched him refuse Richard's invitation to play, and Ellen's to come to art. Nathaniel walked listlessly, aimlessly around the yard, his snake jar cradled in his arm. I walked over to him.

"Think Killer needs fresh grass?" I stooped to pluck a handful.

He looked at me with surprise, then slowly undid the lid of the jar. But Nathaniel didn't want to talk. I sat close by while he, with a long broken branch, outlined snake after snake in the dirt by the driveway. Around each one he quickly drew a circle.

Finally I asked him how he had slept last night at Aunt Josephine's apartment.

"I'm used to stayin' there"—he stared into space—"but I had real bad dreams . . ."

Dreams about robbers who were doing something to his momma. ". . . somethin' to make her look like she was dead."

"You know that's not what really happened to her, don't you, Nathaniel?"

He shook his head and wouldn't look up. "Them robbers musta put them pills down her throat. She never woulda done it herself, never . . ."

"There weren't any robbers, Nathaniel, dear." I moved a little closer to his rigid body, but didn't try to touch him. "Your momma has a kind of sickness—called depression—that made her want to take too many pills. She couldn't think very clearly. But now in the hospital, they'll be able to help her."

He seemed to be thinking. We both stayed quiet several minutes.

"Would you like to send her a message?" The psychiatric unit was the one floor of the hospital children under twelve still couldn't visit. But we could mail a letter.

Nathaniel asked if I would do the writing. "How is you, my momma?" He dictated gravely. "When is you comin' home? I hope they catch them robbers and whip their butts real good till they be dead. I love you, my momma."

He signed it "Nat."

"P.S. If you come back I'll go to bed when you tell me. When you come home I wish you would love me."

"Nat, your momma didn't hurt herself because of you. Depression doesn't happen because a kid won't go to bed."

Nathaniel sat close to me at lunch time, but kept his eyes on Killer and wouldn't talk at all.

After clean-up I explained about the books the children were making. For his, Nathaniel drew page after page of snakes. Snakes in boxes, snakes in jars, "so they can't get out." With each he asked me to write a similar legend:

"He's all alone in his box. He ain't got no family. No one likes him. Because he strikes at other people."

"Killer must be lonesome," I said.

"Uh-uh. He ain't. He can talk to tiny little bugs that you and me don't even notice. An' nobody wouldn't never be sad if we could hear what my snake hears. If we could hear the grass grow."

Rodney went from lunch to "pumping iron." I was frustrated that he wasn't swimming, but his mother had supported his claim of being allergic to swimming-pool chemicals. Usually during his flashy body-building routine he'd turn his head to admire his rippling muscles. Instead he shot nervous glances toward Nathaniel.

He had an announcement, he told Richard, to make at closing circle.

"And when the Big Man talks—" He sauntered to the center of the circle. All the counselors and kids were attentive to Rodney. "Yeah man, when Big Man talks," he repeated, "that's when bull shit walks."

"You're new at this camp, kid." He nodded toward Nathaniel, who looked up briefly, then shrank as small as he could. "Now you don't know me, pal, but Big Man's the name, and friendship's the game. An' I intend to be a friend to you, but I also wanna be a friend to that snake." He pointed. "An' listen, man, I dunno why you keep that critter locked up in that jar, when black people like us," he thumped his chest, "we know what it means to be confined."

Nathaniel hugged the jar protectively, and studied Rodney's face.

"Listen, kid"—he sauntered away from Nathaniel, then suddenly wheeled to point directly at him—"how'd you like to be the one in that bottle?"

"He wants me to take care of him!" Nathaniel screamed, though he crouched even lower. "He likes to be with me! Don't you, Killer?" He kissed the side of the jar.

"Wrong, boy." Rodney shook his head. "YOU may wanna be with HIM but HE didn't get no vote about wantin' to be with YOU."

Tim winced and looked at Nathaniel with compassion.

"Now, I think it's correct to say that I speak for my associates"—Rodney checked each face in the circle like a lawyer surveys a jury—"when I ask you in all fairness"—he paused dramatically—"to give . . . that . . . snake . . . a . . . break!"

Dave and I glanced at each other significantly, agreeing without words to observe this power struggle before deciding whether to interrupt.

"Now, Rich, here"—Rodney flung his arm toward Richard—"he could take that snakie for a nice lo-o-ong ride in his nice old car, wa-ay wa-ay out in the country, right now, this afternoon—"

"No!" Nathaniel stuffed the jar inside his ragged shirt. "Killer stays with me!"

"We'll see." Rodney tucked his thumbs under his armpits confidently. "We'll see about that. I'd like to put this issue to a vote. I'm sure my associates here don't like to see wildlife confined any more than I do. So—I ask on behalf of oppressed and imprisoned people everywhere, all over the whole wide world—who agrees with ole Big Man here? Who thinks this here snake . . . oughta be . . . free? Like me?" His own arm shot in the air.

Gail watched Rodney fondly. Her arm rose too. José's hand got as high as his shoulder before he looked around. Adam's first and fourth fingers darted out in a hex sign—a magical taboo. "As surely as the cosmos stands," Adam said, "his power must NEVER prevail! My energy will absorb his useless flame—"

In his own strange way, Adam had confronted Rodney. José put his hand down. Gail's arm wavered. Her eyes followed Rodney's search for fellow voters.

"You?" Rodney demanded, pointing to Tim, who jumped at being made the focus of attention.

"I think—" He trembled, after a pause. "I think that friends should stay with friends." He raised his head slowly and looked directly at Rodney.

"Look." Rodney shook a fist in Tim's face. "That snake got friends of his own in the woods. Now Rich here could drive him out there like I said—"

"Killer don't go nowhere without me!" Nathaniel screamed in

terror, crossing his arms over the bulge in his shirt that now concealed the jar.

"What about the vote?" Dave interceded. "All in favor of releasing the snake raise your hands."

Not one hand went up.

"Friends should be with friends," Maria spoke softly.

"Prejudiced bastards!" Rodney stormed toward Richard's car. "Slimy Puerto Ricans!"

—— 11 ——

While Richard was collecting his car pool Thursday morning and Bill and Ellen were setting up a balancing beam, I drove over to the Cassones', determined to bring Frankie back to camp. Seven miles along the thruway, then a three-minute ride down a tree-lined side street, past neat little homes of similar bungalow design.

But Frankie's house looked different. The area left of the door was green, but the paint merged at a different spot on every row of shingles with light gray paint that extended across the whole right side of the house. The confusing part for me was that both sides were blistered and peeling. Someone had started fixing the house, but gave up long ago. Funny, I thought, pressing the doorbell, how even houses can looked disturbed.

If the bell rang inside I didn't hear it. Nor did any footsteps respond. Yet I had the eerie feeling that someone was watching and a sense of *déjà vu*, because I'd done all this before—tried extricating children from homes where intervention was unwelcome.

I knocked, called and pounded, then finally went back to my car.

I glanced back and saw one slat of the Venetian blind in the big center window tilted. Yes, the whole blind swayed now, ever so slightly.

I turned off the motor and leapt across the broken flagstone to rattle and bang on the door. "Mrs. Cassone! Frankie! Please let me in—whoever's there! It isn't going to help to hide. Please come to the door!"

I walked around to the back yard, densely overgrown with weeds, to look through the smudged glass on the kitchen door.

Dishes caked with remnants of food were piled in the sink, six chairs and a table buried under mounds of laundry, a pan full of shrivelled peas, a strainer with yellowed macaroni, newspapers, coffee cans. Stacks of papers on the floor. Colored socks, envelopes, opened boxes of crackers on the counters. No wonder Frankie got so fearfully stuck in this place.

I knocked a final time, no longer hopeful someone would answer. Walking away, I decided to file a report to the state division of children's services, charging Frankie's parents with neglect. Neglect, not of their home, but of the emotional well-being of their son.

The state would send a worker to investigate, putting pressure on the parents to get help. Otherwise Frankie would spend another year at home with his mother instead of going to school. The summer was too short for me to try a more conservative route. And I'd grown too impatient.

By the time I got back the children were waiting for opening circle, but I went right inside and phoned Protective Service. I'd have to follow up with a written report and also tell the Cassones a worker would visit their home. But my call to Frankie's father got no further than the university switchboard. The operator had difficulty locating him, and I did not hold on. From the kitchen I could hear Nathaniel screaming.

He'd rested his jar against a tree and run to the barn to give his lunch to Ellen. When he returned, the snake was gone.

The serious search was conducted in teams—one counselor to a small group of children. Ellie's team did the barn. Billy led an expedition through the higher grass by our neighbor's hedge.

Such excitement activated Adam. His hands shot rapid signals of danger—hexes, symbolic slashes across the throat, karate chops to the air. "No time to undertake investigation! Only Thor can sense the proper direction! K-r-rakk! K-k-pow!"

Skipper's behavior suprised me more than Adam's. Instead of trudging along, trying to keep pace with the others, Skipper simply stood across the driveway, watching Nathaniel crying. Dignified Nathaniel was now a pathetic figure, head on his knees as he wept.

Crickets chirped and Millie barked but no one called, "We've found it!" I was thinking we probably ought to quit when Skipper waddled over to Nathaniel, and tapped him on the head.

"Huh? Wha—?" Nathaniel looked up, hopeful.

Skipper tapped him again, then pulled on his arm.

"What—what is it?" Puzzled, Nathaniel rose.

Skipper tugged him toward the toilet.

"I guess he has to go." Someone always had to help Skipper. A good distraction for Nathaniel, who in fact looked pleased at being chosen. I watched him hold the door of the beaten-up old cabinet while Skipper mounted the single step, after several false attempts, by crawling on his hands and knees.

"We found him!" Nathaniel screamed. "We found him!" He burst out the door and twirled down the driveway holding Killer in the jar high above his head. Skipper waddled after him, grinning.

Everyone greeted Killer. The first song at opening circle, "How are you today," was sung to the snake. Nathaniel leaned over to Skipper, beside him, and tenderly helped him stroke the jar.

"How'd that little kid know he was in the bathroom?" Maria wondered, shaking her head.

"Ya, how'd he know?" the kids repeated.

Slowly, Skipper looked around the group. Hesitantly, then faster and faster, he crawled across the circle to Rodney, who began to back away.

"Whatta ya want with Big Man, huh, kid?" he chuckled nervously. "Can I help it if his snake cut out?"

"Pee budder!" Skipper nodded his helmeted head toward Rodney. "Pee budder!" he pointed.

"Beat it, you ugly little freak! Get outta here and shut up!" Rodney whispered harshly.

"I thought so!" Nathaniel leapt to his feet, pointing at Rodney. "I thought he was the one what done it!"

"It's what you get for always grabbin' the window!"

"It's the first day he ever got it, Rodney," Richard answered firmly. "I'll decide who sits where in the car."

"Skipper musta seen him stealing," Carlos observed.

"Hey cool it, man," Rodney shifted to his persuasive voice. "There mighta been some wheelin' an' dealin', but let's not accuse the Big Man of stealin'."

"Kidnapping then," said Carlos.

"Snakenapping," Tim corrected sternly.

"How do you think we should handle this, Rodney?" I asked him.

Rodney saw no reason to apologize. "I was tryin' to teach that punk a lesson." His only regret was getting caught.

The group vote decided his fate. Time out for "at least an hour."

"Prejudiced bastards!" Rodney headed for the time-out chair. Walking by Skipper, he brandished his fist. "Skipper! Your name's a joke! You can't even walk, you ugly little monster."

I met Rodney at the time-out chair. "You, Rodney, you, who talk so much about prejudice, ought to be the last one here to be so cruel to Skipper."

"Sure, Eleanor, talk about what I done! No one ever criticizes what other people done to me!"

"Who? Who's done what to you?"

"Never mind. Besides that little creep don't understand no English." He slouched down in the chair and turned his head away.

Ellen's frantic beckoning caught my eye. I left Rodney under Dave's surveillance and hurried to the second floor of the barn where Ellen was crouched in a darkened corner, holding Skipper. His chest was heaving as though he'd been crying for a long time. Rodney's words may have been unintelligible to Skipper, but his cruelty had been brutally effective.

"I thought I heard someone moving," Ellen said softly, "but the first time I came up I didn't even see him. He must have been hiding."

Ellen, who'd been so repulsed by Skipper, gently wiped his teary face on the tail of her T-shirt. "I'm so mad at Rodney, for hurting your feelings," she said.

"Skipper, you're so brave." I put my arms around them both. "Rodney was mean to you because you weren't afraid to help Nathaniel."

I wasn't sure how much he understood, but Skipper was calmer.

"I'm proud of you too." Ellen gently undid the chin strap on his heavy plastic helmet, whispering words of comfort. She stroked the baby-soft hair and kissed his damp forehead.

"Mom, can I take him to the house to wash his face?"

"Sure, dear."

I watched their progress up the driveway. Graceful Ellie walking haltingly to accommodate the misshapen little boy who clutched her hand.

Just before lunch I noticed Rodney backing Laura against the wall of the garage. She handed him something which he pocketed fast. Dave had questioned them about a similar transaction he saw the day before, but again today they both insisted nothing had happened.

Rodney joined Gail, Maria and me in the kitchen, to decorate the surprise good-luck cake for Laura. Carefully squeezing rose-colored frosting from the tubes, Maria drew before-and-after legs around the vanilla LAURA.

With Dave's help, Gail and Maria smuggled the cake out to the barn. When lunch time was over, Rodney suggested a game in the barn, flashing Dave an elaborate wink, Dave's cue to detain Laura.

"Laura, would you help me put the extra lemonade away?" he asked. She walked beside him delightedly, carrying an almost empty pitcher of lemonade.

We all scampered to the barn, then waited, breathless in the darkness, grouped around the cake.

Maria giggled anxiously.

Rodney demanded silence.

"Shhh! Cool it! She'll hear us."

Lots of heavy breathing.

We heard Dave and Laura's footsteps on the path.

"Hap-birday! Hap-birday!" Skipper suddenly shouted, breaking all the surprise and tension.

Dave grinned at me. This was the only time Skipper had said anything besides "pee budder."

Maria's big dark eyes sprung tears of disappointment. But Laura greeted her cake with squeals. "It really is like a birthday! My new leg is gonna get bornded."

Skipper ate such a big piece and painted his arms and face so well with frosting that Ellen took him to the house for another clean-up before we could let him swim.

Laura stood at the edge of the pool with David, basking in his attention.

On doctors' orders, she wasn't allowed in the water. No last-minute risk of a cold or an infection before her operation.

Rodney worked on a math game with me. He didn't need help with reading, but his number skills were poor, and today he was particularly inattentive.

"What's the matter, Rodney?" I could feel him tense every time he looked toward Laura.

"Nothin'," he shrugged. "Nothin'."

Dave and Laura seemed to be deep in conversation by the post. Suddenly David's voice rose. "He did that to you?" he asked, stepping back from Laura.

"That does it!" Rodney growled, pushing the baseball math game off the table. I watched him tear across the yard—full speed, arms out—toward Laura.

"Dave, turn around!" I cried, and David caught Rodney seconds before he would have shoved Laura into the water.

"You fuckin' bitch!" Though captured, Rodney proceeded to berate her. "You said you wouldn't tell."

"Tell what?" Dave demanded.

"I didn't say nothin' to no one!" Laura huddled as if she were cold. The kids in the pool stopped playing to watch.

"I heard it! Dave asked you if I did it—"

"I was tellin' Dave about my brother! He was tryin' to tease me. I never told no one you made me bring a dollar—"

A pay-off. Protection money. The story all came out, Rodney seething as Laura spilled it. He'd told her he was "magic like a witch doctor" and he could make people die. Or not. He wouldn't cast a spell on her if Laura paid her daily dollar.

Furious, I called an all-camp council, an early closing circle, for everyone to deal with the issue.

"How does that make you feel about Rodney?" I asked, looking round the ring of sober faces.

"I don't believe he's really magic." Nathaniel didn't raise his eyes from the snake jar caught between his knees.

"No one is," Tim ventured, "except maybe Houdini, and he never used it for an evil purpose."

"I want the dollar back." Laura squinted across the grass toward Rodney, flanked by Rich and me.

"The dollar, girl!" he mocked her. "Well, hominy grits an' damnation! I was fixin' to buy me a southern plantation." Rodney looked to Gail for support. She didn't acknowledge the smile.

"Yesterday's dollar too!" Laura said louder.

"Oh no, girl! Now that ain't cool." Rodney slapped his forehead. "Ole Big Man was lookin' to buy me a mule." Rodney's grin froze and faded when Gail returned his wink with a scowl.

"Well? What about what Rodney did to Laura?" Dave rephrased the original question.

"I don't like it," Tim responded.

"I think it stinks," said José.

"Me too," nodded Carlos.

"His-s-s-s—"

"Pee budder."

"Only my stun gun can irrevocably annihilate man's greatest tormentor. Boff! Pow!"

"I think it was mean," Gail said softly. Rodney looked as if she'd struck him. "And I think he's sick in the head."

"So what, girl!" Rodney leapt to his feet. "That's why I'm here!" He bolted up the driveway.

"Come back, Rodney. You're running away from your problem!" Rich shouted.

"Good!" he called back. "That's exactly what I wanna do. An' you can all drop dead! Everyone! The whole damn camp—drop dead!"

He locked himself in Richard's car and made faces through the windshield.

"Don't let it get ya." Diane kept rocking as she spoke to Laura. "My mother says stuff like that to me, but I don't let it get to me."

Diane talked so rarely that everyone was quiet when she finished.

Time was almost up when Carlos suggested Rodney either pay Laura back, or "not be allowed at camp tomorrow."

His brother amended the proposal: ". . . unless he does two dollars' worth of work before he plays."

Laura held out for cash. "So what if he fixes the camp up? I won't even be here."

"She's right," Tim nodded thoughtfully.

Heads turned from Laura to Rodney in Richie's car.

"All right! All right!" Something flew out the window. "I'll give her the fuckin' one spots, ya hear? Stop pickin' on Big Man. The conscience is clear."

Gail scrambled to retrieve the bills for Laura as they blew across the lawn. Then she further disavowed her interest in Rodney by offering a variation of her favorite song.

> *"He's got Laura's crooked l-e-e-e-g*
> *In His hands*
> *He got Laura's twisted l-e-e-e-g . . ."*

Dave put his arms around Laura and Maria. Everyone in the circle linked arms to sing and sway with Gail.

Laura looked adoringly at Dave. "Do—do you—I mean, does anybody wanna hug with me b-before I go?"

"Me first!" Dave swept her up. We all took turns, except Adam, who darted away, and Tim, who offered Laura the four-leaf clover cupped in his palm. "I prefer not to make contact, but I'd be willing to give you this. Originally, it only had three petals, but I taped on a fourth. I believe it should work just as well."

Rodney leaned out of Richie's convertible as Laura passed him on her halting trek to her mother's car. "Don't you trouble to say goodbye to Big Man, cracker, 'cause I ain't gonna kiss you skinny lips."

Laura raised her head coolly and limped by the car without responding, but tripped a few steps later and fell flat out on her stomach. Rodney gasped, "Watch it, girl! You okay?"

Laura got up without a whimper, shook the hair back off her face, and continued her proud march up the driveway.

"See ya, kid," Rodney called. "No hard feelings, ya hear?" He looked back at us pleadingly.

After camp I finally got through to Frankie's father. Yes, he knew his wife hadn't brought his son to camp. In fact he'd taken the car.

"No one came to the door?" He sounded amused till I told him I'd been in touch with Protective Service.

"Look, I know she has problems," he said clearing his throat, "but the older kids all went to school . . . Frankie's bound to start—when he's ready . . ."

No, he couldn't make time for a private meeting, but he'd be glad to bring it up with the group. In fact, indignation beginning to frost his voice, he'd just like to hear what other parents had to say about me calling the state on a private family matter . . . yes indeed . . . he'd be there.

—— 12 ——

I felt too tired to get ready for the meeting without a nap. I fell deeply asleep and woke in a panic. A scary dream about Ann—in Africa—lost and alone.

And barely time to get ready.

In the shower, I thought about Ann and then of Ellen. We'd never talked about her upset over Diane, or my reaction.

I was dashing to my closet when Ellen called me from her tiny corner bedroom.

"Mom?" She was stretched across the bed looking out the window toward the barn. "I've been thinking about Skipper. I didn't realize how much he understood. Rodney hurt him, but so did I, by avoiding him because of his drooling. I'm sorry. I won't do that any more. I'll try to make it up to him."

"He'll be happy about that, Ellie. And it makes me think of the other day when I hurt you." She looked puzzled. "When you were upset by Diane. I want to explain."

"I understand, Mom. I was feeling sorry for myself about never seeing Dad. I guess I wanted your sympathy too, so Diane set the whole thing off. But Skipper taught me something today. If that little kid can be brave, then I know I can. He makes me realize how lucky I am."

"Ellie—" I sat beside her on the old mahogany bed, hers since she was two years old. "Ellie, dear, I'm lucky too."

I felt much stronger, leaving for the parents' group.

I met Nathaniel's Aunt Josephine in the waiting room next to David's office. I was glad she'd come to the meeting.

She wasn't his real aunt, she announced to the group, but since Nathaniel was a baby she took him in when "things weren't fallin' right for his momma. I heard him cryin' the whole night long and I knowed she musta done went an' left him. So I tole that girl next time I seen her, just bring the baby up to me. I be glad to watch him." Nathaniel's mother went out a lot. "Sometime she be gone three, four days at a time . . . never give no explanation . . ." For the past few years Nathaniel took himself upstairs to Josephine.

But Josephine, the newcomer, drew little response from the others. It was Frankie's father who got their attention. He began ranting that I never should have reported them. His wife had problems but it was crazy to call her need to overprotect their son "neglect." If she did too much for Frankie, it was no one else's business.

I heard myself coming on too strong, insisting their not allowing Frankie to become an independent person was severe neglect— emotional, not physical. Every day he stayed at home, every night he spent in their bedroom, reinforced the message that Frankie was helpless—a nothing without his parents. Protective Service could evaluate objectively, providing support and direction to us and the family. Frankie, I concluded, might need more help than any two parents could offer.

"Oh no!" he wagged his finger at me. "We've been through all that before. The school psychologist talked about hospitalization. My wife and I won't allow it! And that worker better not park her damn state car anywhere near our house, unless she wants to be sued!"

"Mr. Cassone"—Dave's eyes met mine with a look I knew meant "let me try." "What's your opinion on how this situation with your son developed? Do you have any theory on why it started?"

"Hmm." The man tapped the bowl of his pipe on a metal ashtray, then refilled it from a leather pouch before he responded. "Yes, I believe I do."

David had bailed us both out. Mr. Cassone could approach the problem intellectually, a route more familiar and comfortable for him.

"My son isn't the only one with fears . . ." he began. "My—uh—

my wife was always frightened growing up. Her mother used to walk her to school but she finally quit school at fifteen. Stayed home till we got married, the year after that. I was twenty-four. Finishing up my Master's degree. At first we lived with her mother—not much of a change for me, since I grew up next door. When we finally bought the house, her mother never missed a day coming over. When she died my wife couldn't take it. She still can't visit her mother's grave."

He told about her anxiety attacks—feelings of panic driving, not being able to breathe when she'd wait in line at the supermarket. Gradual avoidance of places where she had those feelings. "I don't mind doing the shopping." He shrugged.

"Maybe you should mind," Tim's mother said softly. "Maybe that's not really helping. Aren't you doing exactly what she does to your son? Making her feel she's incompetent? That's just what my mother did to me," Tim's mother continued reflectively. "I was the youngest, and she just couldn't let go."

"But that's no excuse to always give in to Tim," her husband interrupted. "Look what you've done to him."

"I hate it"—she looked wounded—"when you make it sound like his problems are because of me. How about the way you talk to him? Maybe that's what's done it."

"Whoa!" Dave held up his hand. "Some people throw custard pies at each other. You two do it with words!"

"Hell," Tim's father chuckled. "What am I s'posed to say to my son? The only compliment my old man ever paid to me was when he was drunk. Before I went in the service he took me into his bar to meet his buddies. And he puts his arm around me. 'This is my son,' he says. That"—he cleared his throat—"that was the closest he ever came to a compliment. An' I was nineteen years old then."

Laura's parents tiptoed in late, having just seen her at the hospital. "A little scared but liking all the attention." Her mother smiled bravely.

"That's all the kid needs," her father added, setting up a folding chair, "getting even more spoiled now. Funny how it's the kids we did the least for—the ones who were on their own while the wife was working—who've turned out best, the most independent."

I hoped that Frankie's father got the message—doing too much for our children is a form of deprivation.

When the others left, I stayed to talk to Dave, mainly about fears, how most of the phobic children we'd worked with were only children in their family, or the youngest. But it was more than position in the family or whether their mothers worked that kept some children stuck. It seemed that some guilt or regret made one parent—often the mother—see one child as particularly vulnerable, needing or deserving special treatment. And the child, perceiving this, learned to wield control, becoming ever more caught in a suffocating web.

Heading home, I wondered why I had reacted so strongly to Frankie's father. Was it because I'd felt what he was feeling? Letting go of my children was hard for me too. Letting go and hoping they were ready.

13

Friday morning, at Ellen's turn to lead the opening circle, the discussion focused on fathers.

"If our father gets along real good with our mother, that's when me an' my brother hate him," Carlos began.

"Not me. I hate him when he hits her."

"I don't got one." Rodney wouldn't pursue the subject.

"Well, mine lives at our house," Maria bit her fingernail, "but I wish he'd go away. When he's mad at my mother, he calls me a baby. Sometimes I still like him, but I wish I always didn't."

Ellie glanced at me significantly.

"My mother hates it that I like my father better. She says it isn't normal." Diane rocked, hands over her stomach. "That's why she screams her head off at me. Diane, you're a slob. Diane, you're a pig."

"You probably deserve it, girl," Rodney interrupted. "What do you think parents are supposed to do? Course they have to yell and whip on everyone."

"Your mother hits you, too?" Gail's eyes widened.

"Course she do, and I deserve it."

"Think that has anything to do with you hitting other people?" Dave asked Rodney.

"No way, man. I just let go like that when I'm mad."

"Our father don't just hit our mother." Maria looked nervously toward her older brothers. "He hits us too."

"We didn't say it before 'cause he'd kill us if we told you," José explained.

"And besides, we didn't wanna hurt your feelings," Carlos added.

Dave shook his head at me. Besides feeling bad for the kids, we both knew what this information meant. State law obliged us to call Protective Service to report suspected abuse.

Tim, who'd said nothing, paused to push his glasses back in place before he took his turn. They'd been sliding down his nose. "I don't care if my parents yell at me," he began. "I get scared when they come home real late from parties and yell at each other. Like last night after the meeting my mother screamed at my father, 'Don't you see what you've done—you embarrassed me, you made a fool of me—'" His voice rose.

"What did he say?" Rodney took a sudden interest in Tim.

"He said he couldn't help it and he thought that maybe he was just a failure."

"Then what?" Rodney edged closer to Tim.

"She said he oughtta get used to that. Then he went out for the rest of the night. But there's a worst part. When he's mad at her he won't even talk to me." Tim began to chew on his fingernails.

"I remember when my father come home one time for a week." Gail nodded as though she could see it. "When he was walking out again my mother say to him, 'Keep movin'. Don't let the door hit you in the butt when you go'."

"One time I found a book of pictures in my mother's dresser." Nathaniel held Killer's jar in front of his face to tell his story. "One is her with a man. An' I held it up to the mirror to see if his face looked like mine. I know I had a father, cause she's got a book about when I was born, got writing on the cover. Says 'Our Baby.'"

"Everyone has a biological father." Tim sighed impatiently.

"Well, me an' Killer want a father to be with. We want a real true family."

"What's so good about real families?" Rodney shrugged, but his eyes were misty.

"It depends on what you call a real family," I said. "When people love each other and try to help each other, I think that's a real family. No matter how many members are in it." I hoped my own kids were listening.

For the rest of the morning, wherever Rodney went there was trouble.

"Rodney!" Ellen called, "the clay stays on the table."

"No!" Rich shouted later. "The bat is for playing ball!"

"Hey, scum dog," Rodney beckoned to Millie, who'd respond to any name for attention. Tim curled up in a ball when she left him to wriggle toward Rodney.

When the boys were changing to swim, Adam ran from the garage stark naked. Arms extended in his super-hero flight position, he leapt toward the pool.

"Boof! K-k-k-k-pow!" He boxed when I caught him. "I must assume a new identity."

Dave walked from the garage with his hand on Rodney's shoulder. "Why you blamin' me, man? 'Cause the kid can't find his swim suit, right? Hey, do I look like a pervert? Now you know that kid ain't wrapped too tight . . ."

Rodney raged on until Skipper waddled to Ellen with Rodney's lunch bag, Adam's red trunks bulging out the top.

Crossing the yard to the time-out chair, Rodney moaned about Skipper. Baby spy. Member of the underground. Only God should have eyes like that kid.

At lunch it was clear that Rodney no longer was accepted as self-proclaimed boss of the world, or even of Camp Hopewell.

His best jokes, coolest raps, even an impressive recitation of major league baseball standings failed to redeem him. Each kid he sidled up to moved away.

Shunned by his former fans, Rodney had no one to turn to but Nathaniel. "Hey, 'bout your snake, man"—Rodney slid closer to Killer—"now if that little critter like dark-skin people like you, I shoulda known he oughtta like me too." Nathanial bit into his jelly sandwich.

"Killer hungry?" Rodney bent forward solicitously. "Little fella like these juicy bugs?" He dangled one between his thumb and finger.

Nathaniel unscrewed the lid and Rodney deposited the insect.

"Say, how 'bout you, Nat?" Rodney held out a little bag of candy. "Want some M & M's?"

Nathaniel guardedly scooped out a handful.

"Take the front seat window going home," Rodney said, clapping his hand on Nathaniel's shoulder. "I don't mind a bit."

It was José's turn to return the pitchers to the kitchen and my turn to accompany him.

I happened to glance out the window in time to see Rodney creeping up to Skipper, who was about to enter the pool.

Rodney held up one finger to Nathaniel, behind him, in a "watch-this" gesture, just before he placed his hands on Skipper.

"Rodney, don't you dare!" I screamed from the window.

But he'd already done it. Skipper tumbled. Dave dove in and caught him the instant Skipper hit the water. The little boy looked more bewildered than frightened.

"Rodney, you brat!" Ellen ran to Skipper with a towel.

I raced down the outside stairs.

Rodney picked up a broken branch and lashed at the water. "Nobody gets away with squealin'—accusin' me, the Big Man, of stealin'."

"Stop!" the children in the pool yelled. "Leave us alone!"

Rodney grinned and again swung the long stick till it struck the water.

"I hate you!" Maria screamed. "You're the meanest boogie in the world!"

"You hear that insult? Git over here, brother Nathaniel, and help me whip up this water! Watch me make them little marshmallows jump! Whe-e-e-e!" He beat the water. "I's makin' honky puddin'!"

Darting and ducking to avoid being struck, Tim and Maria headed for the other side of the pool. Adam, José and Carlos, still less certain swimmers, grabbed the Styrofoam kick-boards to chug themselves across.

Dave boosted Adam out of the pool. One at a time, Rich and Bill reached for the other terrified children. Nathaniel picked up a stick just as I got near them. "Right on, brother Nat, right on!" Rodney exhorted. "Oh-oh." He saw me coming and hurled his stick like a javelin. "Here come de judge! Follow me, man!"

He led Nathaniel down the hill, across the baseball diamond and over the meadow. Rich, Bill and I followed in close pursuit. Rodney and Nathaniel tore through our neighbor's well-trimmed hedge. We broke through behind them but they had disappeared.

"Rodney on the loose!" Bill looked around, shaking his head. "I guess that's all we need."

"Shhh," Rich cautioned. Someone was yelling. Then two figures streaked diagonally across the neighbor's well-tended lawn and burst through another section of hedge, cutting back toward our yard.

Rich and Bill moved fast enough to nab them on the other side. Panting, they surrendered without a struggle. We clutched their wrists and strode across the field.

The rest of the camp inched forward from all directions to meet us.

"Be reasonable about this, Eleanor," Rodney began. "You heard that girl insult my race. You heard her gettin' on my case."

"Just drop the smart talk, Rodney. I'm furious at what you've done."

"Hey now"—he smiled indulgently at me—"bein' mad makes some women cute." He chuckled. "Too bad you isn't one of them, Eleanor." He rocked with laughter.

Nathaniel giggled. Even Bill and Ellen turned away to hide their reactions.

"Hey, really," Rodney said, winking at Nathaniel, "she ain't half bad when she's hoppin' mad."

"Rodney"—I took his chin in my hand—"this is no time to be a wise guy. You close that mouth and I'll do the talking." But I was still short of breath from the chase. "Maria was wrong to call you a name—but think what you did to provoke her!"

"Those kids"—Richard pointed to the ones who'd been in the pool. His cheeks were pale, his forehead and mustache beaded with perspiration. "Those kids did nothing to you—"

"Ya!" Little Carlos agreed, shivering under the single ragged towel he shared with his brother. "You didn't hafta wipe it out on us!"

"Shhh!" his older brother cautioned.

"Look at me, kids," Rodney strutted toward them. José stepped back, pulling the towel away from the scrawny shoulders of his smaller brother. Carlos stood his ground, although his knees were knocking.

"Take a go-o-o-od long look." Rodney stooped to thrust his pugnacious face into Carlos'. With both hands, he stretched the skin around his eyes to enlarge them. "You see one little tear rollin' down my cheek? Now do ya?"

He swaggered back to his original stance between Rich and me. "Now how come you so pissed off, man?" He rested his hand on Richard's shoulder. "Didn't nobody ever tell ole Big Man we wasn't allowed to leave this yard. So look, if we ain't supposed to, me an' my pal just won't do it again, okay? That right with you, ain't it Nate?"

But Nathaniel was running to the tree to retrieve his snake.

"Knock it off, Rodney." Richard shrugged away the tall boy's hand. "You and I both know why you left the yard."

Rodney dropped to his knees. "Don't whup me, massa! Please don't whup me!"

"Then how come you whipped us?" Again little Carlos challenged him, although now his whole body was shaking.

"Shhh!" José stepped forward to clasp his hand on his brother's mouth. "I told you to keep quiet!"

I turned to Nathaniel, who was clutching the jar with Killer inside and grinning at Rodney's antics. "Too bad you'd join in with Rodney when he was taking his revenge on Skipper, who helped you find your snake."

Nathaniel's pleased expression changed to a dark and angry scowl. "Oh no, he did not! That little dopey's the one what took Killer in the first place. That's how come he found him."

Skipper either didn't understand or didn't care. He was patting Ellen's hair as she held him, cozily engulfed in the towel.

"Big Man says he saw him." Nathaniel, his arms across his chest, stuck his nose in the air.

"Uh-uh," Maria countered. "I seen Big Man do it, but I was afraid to tell."

Nathaniel looked from Rodney to Skipper. Rodney saw he was losing his allies. "Lemme at her!" he strained toward Maria, who hid behind Carlos while Rich and Bill held Rodney.

I looked at Dave and pointed to my watch.

"Five minutes to closing circle!" Dave called, blowing his whistle. "Get changed and ready for a very important all-camp discussion."

The girls skipped off to the barn with Ellen, but José and Carlos hung back, shooting angry glances over their shoulders at Rodney and Nathaniel. Richard finally persuaded them to go.

Adam followed with Bill. "Zap! K-k-pow!" His fists pummeled air. "This turmoil cannot cease without my supersonic infinidabulator! Kabloom!"

Rodney tried to assuage Nathaniel with varieties of bugs for Killer. But Nathaniel turned away, picked up Killer's jar and rocked him.

Suddenly the garage door flew open. Out charged Carlos, in dry clothes, followed by José, who yelled directions to his younger brother as they ran across the yard.

"*Matalos*, Carlos! Kill them!"

The smaller boy tackled Rodney, who had no time to get his balance before Carlos began pummeling his body. "We ain't no marshmallows," Carlos raged, "and we ain't no honky puddin'!"

"*Bueno*, Carlos! *Pegale!*" José exhorted, pouncing on Nathaniel.

Maria heard the screams and ran from the barn pulling up the straps of her flowered bikini; then she fell to her knees on the grass and prayed for her brothers—"*En el nombre del Padre, del Hijo y del Espiritu Santo . . .*"

The sudden attack caught me off guard as much as it did Rodney and Nathaniel. I ran toward the wild array of tan and brown arms and legs as the four boys tumbled, wrestled and rolled on the slippery lawn.

Little Carlos got Rodney flat on his back. He sat on his stomach pummeling his chest with flying fists.

"We'll show you—" he cried, an uppercut glancing Rodney's jaw, "we'll show you we ain't no honkies! Me-and-my-bro-ther-is-Puer-to-Ri-can," he shouted, punctuating every syllable with a blow, "and-don't-you-ever-for-get-it!"

"Get offa me, you fucker!" Rodney roared.

With a piercing war whoop Gail dove onto Carlos' back, knocking him off Rodney. "Aww right, girl!" Rodney sat up, shadow boxing. "When in doubt, punch 'em out!"

Maria, beginning her second prayer, *"Padre Nuestro, que estas en . . ."* rose from her knees, and dove onto Gail.

Richard, Bill, Dave and I pulled whichever bodies we got our hands on, but the kids moved so fast we sometimes grabbed each other. It was several minutes before I had Maria. Bill gripped Gail. Rich and Dave restrained Rodney and Nathaniel. Carlos and José stopped punching, but their faces glowered.

Adam paced around us like a referee. "Your retaliation makes the victory sweeter, for you have taken Dr. Doom unaware."

When tempers cooled enough for closing circle, there was a noisy discussion of each person's actions. Skipper sat quietly on Ellen's lap, his face puckered sadly, as he listened to the shouting.

Reprimands were proposed and counter-proposed. "Rodney oughtta be kicked out for good . . ."

"What'd ya think I'd do when your sister called me a boogie?" Rodney demanded of José and Carlos. "Stand there smilin', like dummies in TV commercials?"

I looked at the grass-stained, panting warriors hurling their justifications back and forth, still glaring at one another and restrained only because Dave, my sons and I positioned our bodies between them.

Suddenly I remembered Dave at our first staff meeting, telling his theory on how to passively deflect aggression.

Mockingly, my own voice echoed sentiments about a haven where kids could show us how they really felt.

Theory is one thing, I thought as I swooped to grab Rodney, leaping to his feet again, reality another.

We decided to hold a staff meeting in the old high-ceilinged house, where it would be cooler. We all felt ravenously hungry, the gnawing emptiness I often experienced after a day with needy children. We stayed in the kitchen while Bill mixed up a bowl of tuna with lettuce and tomatoes and Ellen steeped a pot of lemon-mint tea.

Juggling plates and cups, we moved to the rose-painted dining room, to meet as we had before around the oval table. Dave asked how everyone felt "now that we'd survived a second week."

"Ready for a vacation," Richard groaned.

"Today was the pits. At least I hope we've hit the bottom." Bill ran his hand through his sand-colored hair. "I can't believe how fast this started. How quickly Rodney gets out of control."

"I know," Ellie gulped. "My art lesson ended in shambles. You should see the barn. Clay splattered everywhere—all over the floor and walls and even up on the beams. Rodney, Gail and Nathaniel were really awful—dropping globs of clay and making bathroom noises."

"Why didn't you call me, El?"

"I thought I ought to handle the group myself." She looked close to tears.

"But kids regress with clay. It wasn't your fault."

"Now you tell me!" She chuckled as a tear slipped out. "Even Skipper joined them. And Adam—Adam *ate* a chunk of his clay."

"If you were an art therapist," Dave smiled, "you'd call it successful regression."

"Be right back." Richard left to answer the kitchen phone, which was ringing with infuriating persistence.

"Sorry Mom"—he returned to the doorway with his hand clasped over the receiver—"but I think you better take it."

"Harley Parrington here." I didn't recognize the angry voice but knew the name of the neighbor who had moved just a few weeks ago to the road behind ours.

"My wife just informed me of what happened here today."

"What happened . . ." I repeated, trying to grasp some reason for his scathing tone.

"You know damn well!" he ranted. "Or at least you ought to! Don't tell me you're not aware that two kids invaded our property from yours today at two-fifteen!

"My wife just got our four-month-old twins in their cribs for their naps when those two monsters poked their faces right into the nursery window!"

"Mr. Parrington, I'm really sorry. No wonder you're upset. It won't ever happen again."

"Damn right, it won't! 'Cause whatever you think you're doing over there, we're going to end it. Have that bunch of savages in your yard again and I'll complain to the Planning and Zoning Commission and let them stop you for me. We're not paying these kinds of taxes so two wild animals can yell 'Wake up, you little fuckers!' to my babies in their cribs. We didn't move to his neighborhood to put up with that kind of crap!"

"Mr. Parrington, I understand how you feel—only please let me tell you what we're doing . . ." But the receiver slammed in my ear. The dial tone was already buzzing.

"Can't really blame him," Bill sighed softly when I retold the conversation.

"Well, don't worry about him reporting us to Planning and Zoning," Ellen suggested. "Betcha that real estate agent of Dad's already beat him to it."

14

All weekend long I tried to forget about the camp and concentrate on writing. I outlined and re-outlined, then sorted out my cartons of notes the way a dealer distributes playing cards. I knew what I wanted to say, but couldn't seem to transfer the words to paper.

Sunday afternoon Rich and Ellen went to the beach. From my upstairs office I heard Billy moving things around on the porch. I didn't go down to look until after six o'clock, and by that time he was gone. But I found his note on the kitchen counter.

> Dear Mom,
>   The Parringtons aren't our only neighbors! Did a little visiting today to see how the others feel about the camp. The easels, games, rocking horse and assorted treasures on the porch are from the Carlins, the Reisses, the Enrights, Goldhursts, Wieners, Backalenicks, Abbotts, etc. etc. I'll help you sort the stuff early tomorrow morning.
>   Love,
>   District Peacemaker
>   Resident Counselor
>   Your Own Sonny Boy

Monday morning, an hour after camp had begun, the Cassones' car careened into the driveway. Mrs. Cassone got out but Frankie didn't. "I have to be home in an hour." She glared at me coldly. "The social worker from the state is coming to our house. My husband wants Frank to be here."

"Then he'll have to get out of the car." I knew better than to be the one to force him. If I should be able to succeed, it would further alienate his mother.

She knelt on the front seat of the car, pleading with her son, who crouched, both hands covering his head, on the floor in the back. Finally, with all four car doors wide open, his mother walked away. Ten minutes later Frankie flashed from the car to hide behind the toilet.

"You're asking me to die," he screamed when she told him she had to get home. "Is that when you'll be satisfied? You want a kid to die?"

"No, Ma, no!" He pulled on her sleeve as she got into the car. "Don't do it to me, Ma. Don't leave me!" Screeching, he reached through the window to grab her hair. She rolled up the glass, catching his arm till he withdrew it. "Don't go," he sobbed, banging and kicking the car. She began to back away, her face contorted with pain.

Richard and his group got out of the pool to see what was wrong. The children who'd been with Bill and Ellen ran from the barn and stood staring from the driveway.

"At last"—Adam streaked past the car, talking to his opened palm—"at last the moment supreme—"

"How could you, bitch! How could you!" Frankie ran to the road throwing rocks and sticks in the wake of the speeding car. As soon as she turned the corner he collapsed, sobbing, in the driveway. When he glanced up and saw a crowd of anxious children, he half rose, and cowering, scampered to the closest tree.

Rodney tried to master the situation. "What's wrong, kid?" As he swaggered over to Frankie, hands in the back pockets of his jeans, Rodney nodded to the kids who were watching. "Look, I heard ya yelp, and I'm tryin' to help—"

"What's wrong? You fuckin' fool!" Frankie screamed. "That's what's wrong!" He pointed to the empty chair his mother always sat in. "Mother! Mother! Mother!" He pounded and kicked the tree trunk. "Come back! Come back! Come back to me, you crazy, crazy mother!"

The intensity of his rage affected us all. I felt my own heart pounding.

Adam was frantic. "Your feeble efforts at self-preservation cease to amuse me!" His fingers aimed magic hex signs toward Frankie, who began kicking me, Dave and Rich.

"Get away from me, you wicked people! Get away, get away!" he screamed.

Finally, together, we held his arms and legs till he calmed down and promised to sit still. He gasped and sobbed a little longer and then was quiet. The others went on with the schedule.

I reached to console him. "Frankie, I'm sorry you feel so bad. I really want to help you."

He leapt to his feet and tore across the yard directly to the phone. Within seconds he was screeching and cursing.

"Get over here, you bitch, you wicked mother! I'm dying, don't you know that!"

When he slammed the receiver down she called right back. "I'll be there," she gasped.

"No!" I insisted. "Don't come unless I call you." Frankie pulled the phone from the socket and hurled it toward the pavement. It fell apart with a final jangling of bells. Red, yellow, and blue coated wires sprang from the broken shell. Then he ran back to the tree.

"I'm sick of this!" I followed him. "You cannot stay behind that tree!"

"Where am I supposed to go?" he screamed. "Where am I supposed to go, you wicked crazy woman? What am I supposed to do without my mother?"

"Trust me, Frank," I held out my hand. "Trust me for just a little while, as if I were your mother."

"You crazy wicked fool! You're too bossy to be my mother! I'll never trust you or her again—ever."

I waited until his hysterical sobs diminished into body-wracking shudders.

"Listen, Frank," I said, standing over his prostrate form, "the state is at your house because of this situation. Now if you can't let anyone help you, they may think you should go away to a special school."

"Never," he whispered, "never."

"Then here's what you have to do. First, get up and come to the picnic table with me. Then I want you to swim, eat lunch with the kids, play ball, draw a picture, help clean up, come to closing circle and let Richard drive you home."

"You nut! You crazy fool! How could I do all that? The most I can do is sit at the picnic table with you. I could never do any of those other things!"

Drooling like a baby, Frankie spent the rest of the morning at my side. For the first half hour I read to him. When I insisted we join the children who were gathering for lunch, he began to whimper and wouldn't let go of my arm.

When Ellen brought him one of the extra sandwiches we made up each day, Frankie knocked it from her hand. "I can't swallow, you fool! I can't eat," he sobbed, "not—not even if you cut it up!"

Looking troubled, Gail and Maria, who'd been sitting nearest to us, began to edge away.

"And . . ." Frankie spread his hands over his face and wept. "And . . ."—tears were streaking through the opened fingers—"you . . . can all . . . stop calling me a baby!" he cried, " 'cause everybody always wants to call me that!"

"I wonder why you think so, Frank," I said softly. "No one here called you baby."

"Only Triton is able to maneuver under such conditions." Adam, who'd been eating next to Bill, leapt to his feet again, making rapid finger motions as he cried out, "Thak! Zok! Only Triton can locate the helpless human in this ever-changing galaxy." He began to pace around the swimming pool.

"I'm not eating with these maniacs!" Rodney jumped up and stormed away. "The Big Man don't need no nervous breakdown, y'all hear?" he shouted back. "And from the sounds of them two fools the germs is plenty near."

I found Frankie's hanging on to me very wearing. Sniffling and drooling he spent the rest of the afternoon at my side, weeping openly whenever anyone else approached the table. He asked for the model I had once offered him, but shivered and sobbed when I went off to get it.

Bending over the multitude of plastic parts, Frankie studied the directions intently then assembled the silver plane in fifteen minutes.

"What happened . . ." he murmured, gluing on the final wheel, "what happened to the girl with the twisted leg?"

I told him about Laura's operation, that her mother called to say she was doing well and should be back before camp ended. Bill had told the group at opening circle.

"My mother got hurt once." I had to strain to hear him. "She cut her finger on a can."

"Oh? When was that?"

"A couple of years before I was born. She told me all about it."

Now that Frankie was calm, Rodney tried to upset him. "Mother! Mother!" he cried in a high trembly voice, hiding behind a tree. "Come an' save me, Mother!"

Gail, tearful earlier when Frankie cried, ducked behind another tree trunk, copying Rodney.

"Awww ri-i-i-ight, girl!" Rodney gave Gail a thumbs-up salute. "Picking up the Big Man's little torture habits, ain't ya?"

"You've gone too far!" Richard strode over to stop them. "Guess you think you're the only ones here with feelings."

"C'mon, Rich!" Rodney glared. "Why you kickin' on me, man? Eleanor's fat little baby over there always hidin'."

"Ya!" Gail confronted Rich, her hands on her hips. "Pretendin' he scared so he get more attention. So what if his momma be gone. Let him defend for hisself."

"Maaaaa—" Frankie wailed. "Maaaaa!"

"Man! First time I ever heard a squirrel call his momma," Rodney laughed. "Oops, scuse me, fellas." He glanced up the oak tree. "Didn't mean to put you down, brother squirrels. We got lower forms of life down here walkin' earth than any of you four-legged nutcrackers hoppin' in that upper berth."

When Frankie's mother arrived, about forty minutes early, I was tired and more than willing to let him leave. But there was something odd about the tilt of her head, her strange sad smile as she stood by the gate. I wanted to talk to her first.

The boy took refuge in the back seat of their car, urging his mother to get in fast and drive away. But as I walked close to her, closer to the fixed grin and the watery eyes, I realized she was very drunk.

"I, uh, I just didn't want, uh, to see him get hurt." She bowed her head on the wooden fence and cried. "I didn't know what the hell I was doing."

Stumbling, she let me lead her to the old green rocker on the porch. "He's, ah, he's different from those, those other kids . . . I told the worker from the state . . . my—my son was always different. Even—even when he was a little tiny baby, he just wouldn't let me go. I, uh, I hadda carry him with me everywhere I went. It felt like—like there was a growth coming out of my neck."

She wept again and then began to rock herself, holding a handkerchief in front of her face. She was composed enough for me to get her coffee, and as she began to sip she spoke hesitantly about her own fears. She couldn't take an elevator, shop in a crowded store, drive her car on the thruway or over any bridge. She'd been timid as a girl, but since her mother's death the feeling of panic—of not being able to breathe—came more often.

". . . I never thought she'd leave me . . ."

She told her family doctor, who loaded her with Valium. She lost control of her mouth, constantly licked her lips and teeth, made crazy faces.

I felt angry at yet another doctor over-medicating another female patient. Playing god of pills instead of really helping. But her eyes became hooded, distant, as I talked about an alternative. She hadn't heard of Dr. Zane, or his Phobia Clinic in White Plains, New York.

She listened stonily to my telling her that people more fearful than she—agoraphobics, who wouldn't leave their homes—were successfully being treated. Would she trust me? Could I take her to a meeting? She'd have to ask her husband. She had to go now. She stood up and swayed.

I couldn't let her drive. She consented to my driving her car. Richard would follow and bring me home.

She dozed in the front seat. Frankie, having objected to my presence, curled up and whimpered in back. In their driveway she woke with a start, thanked me politely, and walked steadily behind her man-sized overweight son, who dashed to the house to bang and kick on the door.

Gail bear-hugged me when I transferred to the front seat of Richard's car. In the back Rodney and Nathaniel were singing out the

fault that your mother is sick. She can't be with you till she gets well. Can you make a picture of her? Would you show me what she looks like?"

Adam drew Invisible Woman.

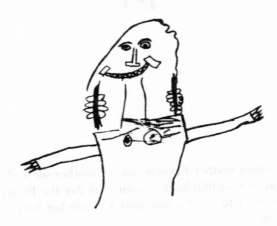

I spent a lot of time with Adam, whose super-hero dolls now collided in mid-air and cascaded to the ground. He played out longer fantasies. A robot woman called Angeroid, who didn't have any heart, pushed men off cliffs, calling vultures in to eat them.

His bizarre behavior frightened the other children. We talked to them about Adam being separated from his mother. Maria expressed compassion. She said she saw the Blessed Virgin "all dressed in white, takin' care of Adam's mother."

Tim withdrew again, curling deep in the bushes. Bill tried to coax him out.

"Get away," Tim whined. "I'd rather be home with my mother."

Rodney tried to comfort Adam. Then, frustrated, he ordered him to "shut up your hand talk," and finally he mocked him, trailing Adam and imitating his frantic gestures.

"Leave him alone!" Carlos said, blocking Rodney. "Let him be, Kunta Kinte!"

"What'd I hear you say? Boy, you lookin' to die today?" Rodney grabbed Carlos. "Learn this, boy, an' learn it quick. I don't allow no references to my roots from no enchilada Spic."

Nathaniel took to hiding with Killer—behind the barn, even inside the house. "Anyone come near us, Killer shoots his poison venom. Just one word from me . . ."

Like Tim and Adam, Nathaniel refused to join the circles, tossing pebbles at kids who did.

Ellen called me over to her afternoon art group. She wanted me to observe Nathaniel. "It scares me, the noises he's making."

Nathaniel bent over his paper, his nose at the end of the pencil, making violent bomb-bursting noises. Explosions. A kid holding so much inside.

I squatted by Nathaniel. "You're pretty angry at the hospital—"

"If they don't let her home real soon I'm gonna get a bomber an' crash the fuckin' place to pieces."

I stayed with the art group the rest of the hour. Nathaniel dropped more bombs on the "hosbiddle." Gail drew page after page of the kind of house her mother might be buying, working contentedly until Skipper crawled into Ellen's lap. "Sure, Ellen, hug the little brat you like so much. Tell him you like his drawin' when you know he only scribbles."

"The old jealousy bit—" Maria suggested and got her hair yanked till I forced Gail to let go.

Thursday night, with Dave's encouragement, I changed my mind about attending Adam's mother's hearing.

His aunt and uncle were distraught. They wouldn't go to the courthouse. They didn't want to see Adam's mother. She'd upset their lives enough already. If she got out, they wouldn't keep the boy another minute. "We don't want her near our house . . ."

"I don't know about you, El," Dave said as he stacked the folding chairs after the meeting, "but I sure need to wind down. Could you stop for a drink?"

"I'd rather get home. Want to sit by the pool?"

Back in our kitchen Dave stirred the iced coffee with a wooden chopstick. He offered one to Bill, who declined with a shake of his head, and passed through the room without a word.

Dave shot me a questioning glance. I shrugged, not knowing why Bill hadn't spoken. I'd ask him later.

We carried the frosted glasses down the steps from the kitchen and over to the webbed chairs by the darkened pool.

Dave sighed as he sat. "Sometimes I feel scared by the kind of talk we heard tonight. So much anger between men and women who used to be in love. I wonder if it could ever happen to Bonnie and me. It's been so good—"

Suddenly all the floodlights Billy had mounted on the back of the house, the trees, the barn, glared on us simultaneously. For a moment, I couldn't see.

Dave squinted at the brilliant floodlights. "Guess someone in there doesn't want me sitting with his mother . . ."

Bill came back into the kitchen after Dave left.

"What's wrong, Bill?" I touched his shoulder and felt him pull away from me. "It's been a hard week, hasn't it." I looked at his drawn face. Adam's upset had triggered days of chaos.

He picked up his book and headed for the stairway. "I just don't feel like talking."

Friday morning Bill was cheery. After camp he was taking the train to Boston to see his girlfriend. He told the kids at opening circle he'd be going away for the weekend.

"Woo-woo, Bill!" There were shouts and giggles. Except from Gail, who angrily muttered a shocking comment. "Bet he kiss her on the bottom way. Not just the top."

I waited until the children settled into activities before departing for Adam's mother's hearing. Ellen was helping Skipper, Tim, Diane and Maria make birdhouses by gluing popsicle sticks together. Dave was showing Carlos and José how to dive from the edge of the pool. Rodney, Nathaniel and Gail were praticing soccer kicks with Richard. Bill, his back against a tree, cupped his hand over Adam's fingers to teach him to strum the guitar. Adam kept a fixed grin, but his eyes were far away.

I felt comfortable about leaving, and enjoyed the trip through the countryside, past grazing cattle, rolling hills, acres and acres of corn and finally along the narrow road into Fairview, where it turned out to be "Sidewalk Summer Sales" day.

The downtown streets, closed to vehicles, were crammed instead with pedestrians. Forced into a stream of traffic, I grew so anxious about getting to the hearing that I parked in a space marked "Municipal Employees."

"Will my car get towed?" I called to a well-dressed man whose briefcase made me hope he was a lawyer and could direct me to the courtroom.

"Parking tickets here cost exactly one dollar"—he smiled—"the only fact to recommend Fairview . . ."

Yes, he'd show me the courthouse. He was going there also.

I passed through the swinging doors marked "Probate" and took a chair in the small square waiting room, opposite a jittery man and a white-suited attendant.

Watching them, I wondered about Adam's mother. Would she be able to care for her son if the judge decided to release her? Adam's social worker had called her schizophrenic and said she lacked the necessary anxiety that prodded people to try to get better.

What a strange disease, I thought, that afflicts one percent of the world's population, regardless of life style. People in jungles, high-rise apartments and dirt-floored shacks like Adam's mother. Was schizophrenia her response to pressure, just as some of us develop ulcers or asthma?

Suddenly the door marked "Courtroom A" swung open, and a man holding a sheaf of papers called, "Susan Bentley."

From an anteroom I hadn't noticed, a tall man in a three-piece suit guided a thin young woman through the waiting room. One thick, shiny black braid cascaded down her back. Heavy black eyebrows and wide green eyes like Adam's dramatized her pale oval face. The tail of her gauzy embroidered peasant blouse hung over her long multicolored skirt and she was barefoot.

I followed, expecting to enter a traditional courtroom, but found instead one long conference table, oak armchairs at the ends, three more chairs along each side.

"We're meeting today," said a large white-haired man with sunken cheeks, rapping a silver gavel, "to consider a petition for Susan Bentley's release from the state mental institution at Fairview. All present please identify yourselves to the court stenographer. I am Judge Polanski."

The psychiatrist, the social worker and the lawyer gave their names to the woman bent over a small machine at an adjacent table. When the judge looked at me, I added my affiliation with the child guidance center and my work with Susan Bentley's son. Adam's mother stared straight ahead, her hands clenched in fists. Not a flicker of interest in my presence.

After the names were recorded, the judge turned to the psychiatrist. "How do you find this patient?"

"Gravely disabled, Your Honor."

"On what do you base your finding?" the lawyer asked, leaning across the table toward the doctor.

"On two psychiatric evaluations and extensive reading of the patient's record. She evidences no insight about her behavior. Her judgment is gravely disabled. She tries to displace onto others the blame for her own behavior. She fails to recognize that she requires treatment, fails to realize it is necessary to her life and to the quality of life for her son, whom she has often abandoned."

"In what sense is she gravely disabled?" the lawyer persisted.

"She places herself in dangerous risk-taking positions such as"— the psychiatrist flipped through a folder of papers—"being sexually assaulted and beaten after taking rides from strangers. She's been in emergency rooms five times since September after police have found her incoherent."

"Are these episodes drug-related?" The judge looked at Susan, who smirked.

"Some." The psychiatrist nodded. "She admits to taking acid. But it's no longer possible to determine whether her psychotic episodes stem from drug use. And it doesn't really matter. Functionally, she's schizophrenic."

"Susan," the judge said, turning from the doctor, "if we release you today, will you avail yourself of help and medication for your problems?"

"My only problem"—she glared at him—"is being locked up by fuckin' assholes."

"Have you ever been employed?" the judge interrupted.

"I don't have to work." She grinned. "The government gives me money for bein' crazy."

"Will she ever improve?" The judge turned back to the doctor.

"If she would cooperate and avail herself of help."

"Fuck you!" she raised her middle finger at the doctor.

"Susan," the judge began kindly, "to refuse to help yourself would not be a rational decision. If that's your choice, I must assume you need protection."

"Fuck you too, Your Honor!" She rushed toward the door.

The lawyer grabbed her and tried to calm her down, the same way we held Adam.

His mother rolled her head and bit the back of his hand.

Outside the courthouse a van marked "Fairview Hills" waited at the curb.

I was about to return to my car when I saw a ruddy policeman leading Susan Bentley to the wagon. "Take care now, honey," he said, and supported her elbow as she hiked up her skirt to climb the step.

Ignoring the seats, she dropped to the floor, cross-legged. The policeman waved. Adam's mother raised her middle finger in a final gesture of defiance.

Adam, Adam, Was there any hope for Adam? Had the damage already been done? Had his mother been using drugs while he was forming in her body? Seeing her so childlike and dependent, I understood her son's retreat into fantasies of omnipotence. No wonder Adam cried for Invisible Woman.

Camp was over by the time I got home but Richard and Bill came out to the porch to tell me what happened.

After I left Adam got frantic, hammering his head against the tree, scratching at his eyes, even putting his hands around his throat to choke himself. Nothing would calm him. They tried to call his aunt. She wasn't home.

Rodney grew agitated watching Adam. At first he tried to talk to him, but Adam acted as if he didn't hear. As Adam lost control, Rodney got more anxious and finally angry.

Adam paced around the pool. Rodney blocked him. Adam turned to walk in the opposite direction. Rodney elbowed him into the water. Adam, fully clothed, sank until he was rescued by David.

They isolated Rodney, who kicked and spat.

At lunch time, when Adam was on the driveway near the barn, Rodney dropped a thirty-pound cement block from the second-floor window. It missed Adam's head by inches.

"It could have killed him," Bill said. "We just can't keep a kid like that."

I needed time to think, despite the crisis.

"He shouldn't come back, Ma," Richard eyed me. "Rodney tore the place apart before he left. Splashed paint all over the art room—wrecked the tables—it's a mess."

"Well Ma, what do you think?" Bill pressed. "Dave agrees with us—and you would too if you'd been witness to his violence."

"Please"—I held up my hand—"I'm too tired to make that decision. But I feel as though we'd be missing the point of the camp to be giving up on Rodney."

"Giving up! He's a danger to the others!"

I went upstairs knowing I wanted Rodney to come back.

An hour later Bill pounded on my door. Had I moved his wallet? He'd left it on the piano and now it wasn't there.

Richard was waiting in the kitchen to drive Bill to the train for the long anticipated visit with his girlfriend. The round-trip tickets and thirty dollars Bill had saved for the weekend were in the missing wallet.

Rich, Bill and I dragged the piano away from the wall. A piece of sheet music. Several dust balls. No wallet.

We looked under cushions, high on book shelves, in the piano bench and finally in places where he hadn't even been.

If they didn't leave, Bill would miss the train. Rich and I pooled twenty-five dollars. I offered to write a check for his ticket. But Bill knew our financial situation, and wouldn't take it.

Time ran out. He called his girlfriend to say he wouldn't be coming. Then he went off for a walk alone.

Too tired to get up, too troubled to rest, I stared at the ceiling until I thought I heard Bill's footsteps on the porch.

"C'mon up, dear." I called.

"You really mean that?" a stranger responded.

I almost tumbled, rushing down the stairs. "I thought you were my son!"

"Delivering this for the P and Z." He grinned, shoving an envelope into my hand. "Sign here."

"Sorry I'm not your son." He waved, turning to leave.

I sat on the bottom step to open the envelope. An official notice to cease and desist our violation of zoning regulations.

Maybe it was just as well.

All evening, all the next day, I was torn between waging a battle against the ruling of the Planning and Zoning Commission and giving in and closing in a week.

Our arguments about Rodney, the theft of Billy's wallet, word from the agent that he had a potential buyer, my own discouragement about not having time for the family work so needed with the kids who were coming to camp, made me question the value of going on.

Richard and Ellen were surprised that I was indecisive. "It's not like you, Ma. You can't disappoint the kids."

"What does Dave say?"

He came over Sunday morning for a meeting. Billy chose not to attend, and sat out on the porch while Dave, Rich, Ellie and I talked about options.

In twenty minutes we knew what to do. Better to face the consequences of violating zoning that let down kids we hoped were learning to trust. Dave decided to tell the parents the problem, just in case.

We started to end the meeting with handclasps. Instead, we hugged each other.

Dave and Rich went out to vacuum the pool. Ellen and I lugged sponges, a pail of water and brooms to tackle the mess Rodney had made of the area she used for art.

We washed the tables, reorganized paper, crayons and scissors and repacked clay in plastic garbage bags to keep it moist. The paint Rodney had splattered had ruined most of the pictures and artwork Ellen was displaying. We took them down. The walls looked bare but the barn was clean. Ready to begin again.

I carried the tall yellow wastebasket of discarded materials to the garbage cans outside the garage. Transferring the contents, I noticed something rectangular and brown.

"Oh God, Ellie! I just found Billy's wallet! The money's gone. His tickets are still inside."

Bill was in the dining room writing a letter. He looked through the wallet with his lips drawn taut. "Is Rodney coming back?" he asked.

"Bill, we have no proof it was Rodney. You said yourself all the other kids had access to the house on Friday. I'd like to keep him out on one-day suspension, Monday, then take him back with conditions."

"Tell him I want my money back."

"You know I can't accuse him."

He turned back to his letter.

"Bill, I know you're disappointed about the weekend."

"It's more than the weekend." He didn't look up. "Nothing's turning out the way I expected. I'll stick with the camp until you get a replacement but then I'm going to Boston."

"What can I say, Bill—please, don't leave this way. Let's try to work things out."

"Did you give Dad a chance to work things out?"

"There are things between your dad and me that you don't understand, Bill!"

"I understand enough, Ma."

"But Bill—there's no comparison! Your dad is a grown man—a man who's been very successful. He's not a helpless tormented black boy."

"Please leave me alone. I've made up my mind."

16

How was your weekend?

—Our father knocked our mother down.

—She said it mighta hurt the baby.

—I hope he burns in hell.

—Carlos! *No digas eso! Silencio!*

I listened, thinking how close we'd come to closing.

—My father stayed away. My mother thinks he likes another woman. Camp Dog, where are you?

—Zap! K-k-k-pow! I must recycle the force beam. Turn into a substance able to withstand a million pounds of pressure! Varoooom!

—Pee budder.

—Next week I go to court. Then I can live with my mother. I already got my bag packed. It's right beside my bed. The Bennetts can't do no adoptin'.

—My mother said it wasn't natural for me to want to see my father. I hate her! And my stomach hurts. So leave me alone. All day.

—My mother comes home tomorrow! Me an' Killer won't be comin' back.

—Why you two can't come back? So what if your mother be home?

—No way! Think we're gonna give them robbers another chance to hurt her?

"I didn't have much of a weekend, either." Billy's turn after Nathaniel. "Remember I was going to Boston to visit a friend?"

"Your GIRLfriend!" Gail corrected.

"Yeah, well it didn't work out. My wallet was missing. Got it back on Sunday, but all the money was gone."

"Who ripped you off?" Carlos leapt up, shadowboxing. "Lemme at him."

"I dunno." Bill shrugged, looking around. "If anyone's got any ideas, I wish you'd tell me."

"Uh-uh."

"If I knew I'd kill 'im."

"Sorry, Bill."

Expression of sympathy. Adam's and Skipper's uncomprehending yet compassionate stares. No overt indication of guilt or tension.

I was glad Bill didn't add that he was leaving. Maybe there was still some hope.

Activities began. Another warm cloudless summer day. I watched Dave's early morning group, the kids who'd come to camp nonswimmers, springing off the diving board. Richie conducting a special "Frisbee clinic." Bill with José, Diane, even Adam, taking turns plucking chords on the guitar, beating rhythm on tambourines and bongos. Ellie's kids glazing their sculptures. She'd found a kiln to fire them. I heard her urge Nathaniel to finish molding his family of snakes.

"Why should I? I won't be back to get them." He went to art, but Nathaniel was nervous and edgy.

At eleven I stopped my reading lessons to bring him inside with the group making Jell-O and brownies. He stirred the Jell-O right out of the bowl, ate the brownie mix, cursed when it was Skipper's or Maria's turn, begged for apples, orange juice, crackers.

"Nothing fills us up. Right, Killer?"

Nathaniel wouldn't sit still at lunch. He ducked behind trees, making faces, eager to be chased. I led him upstairs to the barn, but he was too jumpy to talk. He spread a box of model parts all over the table, then couldn't put the plane together.

"It must be hard, Nathaniel, to be waiting for your mother."

"Hard?" he screamed, "hard? It's ain't so hard—it's easy!" He ran around the room collecting the assorted chairs. Some Nathaniel folded and carried. Three were so heavy he had to drag them to the corner where he lined them all up, two in a row, five rows of pairs.

Then, on the backs of two cardboard cartons he Magic-Markered a lot of knobs, gauges, dials, and stacked the boxes in front of the first row of chairs. He was calmer now, working on this project, and seemed not to care that I was watching.

One by one he placed stuffed animals—Billy's old tiger, a bean bag frog, a teddy bear—on the second to fifth rows of chairs, ignoring the many dolls.

Before he sat down, Nathaniel strapped on a football helmet. Then he and his snake took seats behind the cardboard panels. Nathaniel held the Magic Marker to his mouth like a microphone.

"This is your captain. We're out on the runway . . . we're takin' off . . . rrrrr—v-room! We're flyin'!

"Oh-oh." He leaned to the left, then far to the right. "Oh-oh. Sorry to tell ya. All the engines are burnin'. We're gonna crash! We're crashin' . . . crashin' . . . crashin' . . ."

He kicked the cardboard boxes, which flew as he knocked over all the chairs and occupants. Grabbing Killer's jar, Nathaniel dove to the floor.

Silence. Not a word. No movement.

Slowly, cautiously, he began to stir, lifting his head just inches from the wood.

"Nope." He looked around. "There ain't no survivors."

Nathaniel collapsed on his snake.

At closing circle Nathaniel carried Killer around, holding the jar in front of each person's face. Maria blessed the snake. Skipper tapped the glass and giggled. Gail said, "I'll be going soon, too." Hissing, Adam did a writhing kind of dance, with finger signs to Killer. Tim asked Nathaniel for Killer's classification.

Nathaniel smiled and rocked as kids and counselors sang farewell:

> *Goodbye, Nat. Goodbye, Nat.*
> *We hate to say Goodbye, Nat.*
> *Goodbye, Nat. Goodbye, Nat.*
> *We like you very much.*

But just as the circle was breaking he asked to take home a model for every day he'd be missing.

"Sorry," Bill responded. "The models belong to the camp."

"You may keep the one you started," I said, "and we could wrap the extra brownies—"

"Keep your ugly brownies!" He stormed away.

I was glad to see Nathaniel smiling from the back seat of Richie's convertible as I stood in the driveway waving.

I was still calling goodbye when a friend of Billy's sped through the gate on a ten-speed bike.

"You remember Bob, Ma? He might be interested in taking my place, so I wanted to show him around. He's worked with kids before."

Disappointed, angry, I went inside to dress for the clinic and lathered so much shampoo in my hair it was hard to wash it out. I was still under the shower when Richard banged on the bathroom door.

"Hey Ma!" he yelled. "How come you let Nathaniel take home so many models?"

"But Rich—I didn't!"

Richard dropped me off at the clinic. Because they didn't have a phone, he was driving to Rodney's to let him know he could come back to camp—conditionally.

I had every hour scheduled from four to closing time at nine, but before seeing any clients I called Protective Services and railed about Frankie's continued absence. When would the worker go back to the Cassones? I knew how overworked they were. I knew I sounded demanding. But Billy's quitting, Nathaniel's taking off with the models—I was tired of being patient.

The first appointment was an "intake"—people new to the clinic—a haggard woman, thirty-five years old, whose stockbroker husband beat her so often, so severely, the police held a warrant for his arrest. She insisted on dropping the charges. "I'm the only one who understands him . . ."

She'd brought her withdrawn ten-year-old, who'd witnessed much of the violence.

No time to think about Richard's mission till he picked me up at nine and spilled out details driving down the Post Road.

Rodney had greeted Rich on the porch of his rickety multifamily tenement. He extended his arms and refused to let Richard pass, yelling, "Now you're the one who's gonna get your feelings hurt!"

His mother burst angrily through the door, charging Rich with picking on her son. "How come Big Man the only one be caught?"

Rodney stood behind his mother, imitating her, wagging his finger at Richard, who tried to explain that Rodney was the only one who pushed kids in the pool and dropped a cement block next to someone's head.

His mother remained unconvinced and defensive. Rodney had tapped Richard on the shoulder. ". . . stop kickin' on my momma."

"I think we're taking a risk, Ma," Rich said, turning to me at the stop light, "giving that kid a second chance . . . yet I felt sorry for them both. The tenement they live in is nothing but a firetrap. No fire escape. The stairs are broken. Roof sags in. At first I thought the building was abandoned."

Jack Fuller, director of the Housing Authority, had referred a lot of cases to our clinic. We'd always given him prompt action. So I didn't hesitate to phone him, although Rich and I got home at ten P.M.

". . . sure I know that place," he responded. "Your son is right, it *is* a hell hole. But it's also a multifamily dwelling and there's not one other unit in town for any of those tenants . . .

"Sure, it's immoral. It's one of the most immoral things we do. Turning our backs on unfit housing that ought to be condemned. But what's our choice? If we push on the landlords they abandon the buildings. No matter how these people live, they're better off than they'd be on the street."

17

Richard brought Rodney back to camp.

Nathaniel arrived by taxi an hour after we began and streaked from the car, Killer under his arm. "Bitch! Bitch!" he screamed. "I hate her! I hate her!"

Nathaniel tore around the yard, yelling obscenities till I caught him and the story poured out with tears of rage. Josephine had forced him to come. She wouldn't let him wait for his mother outside the locked apartment.

"What if she be there without me and—and—she don't know where I'm at?" he yelled in my face.

"Nathaniel, don't worry. Your mother knows you come here."

Dave invited Nathaniel to swim. Leaving me "in care of Killer," he ran to change. But the group was still in the water when Nathaniel returned, shivering and dripping, pleading to use the phone.

Wrapped in my towel, he dialed and redialed, every time getting the same recorded message ". . . the number you have called is not in service . . ." But Nathaniel insisted he was dialing wrong.

Finally he urged me to call the hospital. "Maybe nobody wouldn't let her go."

"She was discharged this morning at ten A.M." the unit nurse reported.

"Woop-eeee! She's home! She's home! My mother's home!" Nathaniel couldn't contain his elation. Holding Killer aloft, he ran around the yard screaming out the news. Back to me for a hug. Down the driveway for a hug from Ellen. Hand slaps with Rich, Bill and Dave. Double slaps with Rodney. "Awww riiiight, man! Hey— I'll write her a poem, say I'm glad she be home."

Nathaniel drew a snake-in-the-circle card. Rodney's showed the Fonz on a motorcycle leaping over seven burning cars. Maria Magic-Markered rainbow-colored rosary beads. Gail wrote "Glad you be back, I'm not home yet, but I will be soon. I love you."

Nathaniel left cradling Killer's jar in the shoe box full of greetings for his mother.

18

"Nathaniel's in the car!"

"His mother still ain't back yet!"

Rodney and Carlos shouted the news from Richie's convertible before it came to a halt.

The children tumbled out, and ran to the barn with their lunches and swim suits. Everyone but Nathaniel. Rich stood at the open door talking into the car that seemed empty until Nathaniel yelled, "Fuck off! Leave me alone, Rich! Come any closer an' Killer gets the signal. An' in case you don't remember, Killer's a computerized snake! He never forgets my enemies!"

Rodney swaggered back up the driveway, his thumbs tucked under his armpits. "Let Big Man handle this one, Rich. That kid done blown his trigger. So what if you ma ain't comin' home? Get out, you little nigger!"

"I don't need that kind of help." Richard held up his hand, keeping Rodney away. But Nathaniel squirmed under Rich's arm and ran down the driveway screaming, "I'm gonna bomb that fuckin' hospital! I'm gonna kill that fuckin' doctor!"

"I'll get him." Bill put down his guitar. I was glad he wanted to go. I sat with Adam, Skipper, Gail and Diane under the maple tree, ready for opening circle.

"Hey, look! What's that?" Gail pointed to something falling from the upper level of the barn. Nathaniel bent out the window to watch it tumble. "You wanna die, bitch? I'll kill you! I'll kill you!"

He dropped the next doll by its hair, then the lifesized baby. Rag dolls, plastic dolls careened, twisted, somersaulted from open window to blacktop pavement.

Some blew apart on impact. Arms and legs flew off. Heads rolled from torsos, bouncing to a halt. Others convulsed and lay still. One landed intact on the grass.

"Ohhh, my babies!" Maria blessed herself. "My babies!"

I raced down the driveway as Nathaniel appeared again, carrying a big cloth doll Ellen had made. "Bitch!" He shoved it through the narrow window. "Die, bitch, die!"

Feet first, the flexible doll descended in slow motion, jerking grotesquely halfway down the side of the barn, a rope around its twisted neck. Nathaniel held the other end, battering the doll against the blacktop then yanking her up again and again. Her yellow yarn pigtails caught on the rough clapboard, ripped from the beige cloth scalp, and dangled on their own. "You wanna die—I'll do it for you! Die! Die! Die! Die! Die!" Nathaniel screamed at the bald doll, hanging limply.

"*Madre de Dios!*" The three Hernandez kids knelt down.

Tim scurried off to hide.

Skipper wailed and waddled to Ellie.

Adam went berserk, screaming as he ran beside me. "Thoom! Zak! Don't you feel it? The whole galaxy is shaking! K-pow! K-splunk! All so hopelessly lost!" He began to tear at his face with his fingernails, until Dave and Richie caught him. But Adam's cheeks were bleeding.

I saw Bill at the window latch on to Nathaniel and haul up the doll. I tore up the ladder stairway, but stopped halfway, as soon as I saw what was going on.

Nathaniel was pounding on Billy's chest, but he was small and Billy could control him. Something warned me not to intrude.

"Mother fucker!" Nathaniel shrieked, fists flailing. "You motherfuckin' mother fucker! I hate you—hate you—hate you! Why? Why? Why? Why didn't you come home? You mother-fuckin' mother!" Clutching Billy's neck, both thumbs at his throat, Nathaniel screamed, "You mother fucker you! You mother! Bitch! Mother! Bitch! Mother! Mother! Mother—mother—mother—mother." He collapsed in Billy's arms.

He cried, desperate wracking sobs. "Maaa, ohhhh Maaaaa . . ."

"It's okay," Bill whispered, stroking the tight black curls, the heaving little body. "It's good to cry, Nathaniel. Let it all come out."

The keening wails slowly faded to sporadic gasps. "I know how it is"—Bill rocked him—"to feel real angry with your mother."

· Nathaniel's thumb found its way to his mouth.

"I felt like that too." Bill looked out toward the window, "but you know what I think now, Nat? Maybe there are things about our moms that you and I don't understand."

Nathaniel slurped on his thumb, his face against Billy's chest. I didn't want to interrupt them, so I tiptoed down the stairs.

He was calm at lunch time, able and willing to respond to Rodney. "Hey, man. How come you made them dolls go splat? 'Cause you nervous where your momma's at?"

"I thought she musta died an' nobody didn't tell me." Everyone watched Nathaniel, but he kept his own eyes lowered. "Only Josephine tole me she run away. I think she hates me. Else she might woulda come home."

David cleared his throat, breaking the heavy silence. "If that's true, Nathaniel, it means there's something wrong with your mother, not with you. You're a lovable kid. I know because I love you."

"Me too," Bill nodded gravely.

"That don't make no matter," Gail scowled, her hands on her hips. "So what if you love him but his mother don't?"

"Well, I agree with Dave." I looked around at all the serious faces. Rodney biting his nails. Adam rolling his eyes. Tim peering through horn-rimmed glasses. "There's something wrong with grownups who don't know how to love their children. Some reason they never learned how.

"I think it's sad and unfair if kids are born to people who don't know how to act like mothers. But it's never the kid's fault. And I feel sorry for any mother who'd be missing a chance to love a person like you, Nathaniel. Or Gail. Or any one of you."

Rodney nodded somberly. Gail sucked her thumb. "Our mother loves us . . ." Maria whispered.

Adam began to wander away. "Zap! K-k-k-pow! In the name of the galaxy, what have they done with Wonder Woman?"

Frankie's father had had a call from "YOUR state worker. I let her know my wife and son have stomach upsets. When they recover, he'll be at camp."

"I imagine they'll be well by Monday," I ventured. "Let's try something new, Mr. Cassone. You bring Frankie—Monday."

David shook his head and slumped back in his chair when they left. "Do you realize what went on here tonight? Everyone pursuing his own agenda with little concern for each other—like the kids at camp."

"Last night I talked to someone who cares a lot about you," I said to Gail, thinking of her foster father.

"Huh!" her eyes bore through mine. "I know what that mean, Eleanor." She put her hands on her hips. "That means you be crazy, 'cause if you been talkin' to someone who care a lot about me, girl, you been talkin' to no one!"

"Hey, Gail, you know that isn't true. Right here in this yard a lot of people care."

At circle time, while Bill played guitar, Gail crept behind me to administer a bear hug so startling that we both toppled over.

While I was reading with Maria, she threw a folded paper on the table:

Her note and its delivery reminded me of foster kids who came to the clinic ready to profess their love to every stranger they encountered. The receptionist, the bookkeeper, the psychiatrist, even the custodian got messages from needy kids.

I beckoned to Gail, to hug her on my own terms—gently—face to face.

When Maria skipped off to swim, Gail leaned across the table on both elbows, her nose just inches from mine. "Hey, Eleanor. Ya wanna play a game?"

A reversal of her good mother–bad kid game. "You be the nice, nice kid an' I'm the wicked mother. Make pretend you like me but when I drink beer I'm mean. Mmmm, best beer I ever tasted." She guzzled from an invisible bottle. "Now get over here! Do what I tell you!" Gail scribbled a multicolored list of duties:

"Being your kid is not much fun," I protested.

"You rather be locked in a closet? You want I should give you away? Well then, shut up an' do it!"

"My mother'd never let anyone have us." Maria, sunning after her swim, raised her head from the towel to look off in the distance. "She hugs us all the time."

Diane, leaning against a tree, looked up from her sketch book.

"When I was little I tried to hug my mother. She said I wrecked her makeup."

"Well, no mother would really give her child away," Tim observed from the shady bush where he was grooming Camp Dog.

"Listen, boy." Gail chose Tim for her scapegoat. "You think that what she wanted? You think she gave us kids to the state?" Gail snatched the comb from his hand. Tim tripped, backing away, and landed on his bottom as she waved the comb in his startled face. "Then why would I be goin' to court?"

"I don't know about your particular mother." Tim winced. "Maybe she's an exception."

Gail cocked her head in a puzzled manner, then dropped the comb on Tim's chest. "Well, all right then!" She strutted away.

Gail played demanding mother to my obedient kid while across the pool Nathaniel arranged the deck chairs in rows of two for his airplane game. He and Killer sat in the front seats behind the cardboard panel.

"This is your captain," his voice carried over the water. "Sorry to repeat—this plane is hijacked. Bang bang!" then silence.

Gail was ordering me to "change that baby's filthy diaper!" when Nathaniel spoke again. "Sorry to have to say we lost our motors an' both our wings are breaking off. We're crashing—crashing—crashing . . ."

Nathaniel hit the grass with Killer as someone tapped my shoulder. Startled, I turned to face a tall gray-haired stranger in blue denim skirt and pink striped blouse.

"Catherine Sexton," she said, extending her hand. "Planning and Zoning."

My heart took a plunge. Could she close us down, right now? I looked at Gail, edging away from the woman, at Nathaniel playing dead, at Ellie and her kids making windmills, Rodney handing Rich the basketball, Dave encouraging Skipper to float, Billy comforting Tim . . .

"You know that you're in violation." She drew an envelope from her purse. "How long did you plan to run this camp?"

"Only four more weeks." I tried to smile, aware of Dave's anxious glances and of Adam circling around us, talking to himself and shooting magic finger signals at the intruder, who glanced at him uneasily.

"We won't be having it here again. I have to move. I'm sorry about the violation, but I didn't have any choice." I heard myself prattle. "Let me tell you what we're doing."

Gail placed herself between us, then flicked a folded paper at Mrs. Sexton, who failed to catch it. Gail bent to pick it up, handed it to the woman and disappeared. I was annoyed at Gail's interruption.

"To a beautiful lady," Mrs. Sexton read, "I love you, I love you."

"Thank you, dear." Mrs. Sexton looked around for Gail, who'd disappeared behind the outhouse.

"About the camp—" I began again.

"I already know," she held up her hand. "We've had a batch of mail from parents, and some from your neighbors. But I can't let testimonials interfere with my duty. However"—she paused to tuck the long envelope and Gail's note in her shoulder bag—"I, uh . . . I . . ." She shaded her eyes and glanced around the yard. "I do need time to prepare the final notice. And then my secretary will be on vacation. Nooo . . . I don't see how we'll get it typed and out to you before the end of August. Now—uh—does that sound fair?"

"Oh very fair, Mrs. Sexton!" I grinned and pumped her hand. "Thank you!"

"Off the record"—she bent her head toward mine—"we're mighty proud to have this camp in our town."

Walking to her car, Mrs. Sexton blew a kiss to Gail. And so did I.

There were rumbles of thunder and a darkening sky as we cleaned up the yard. Even though the kids had to help, there were always towels, unclaimed underwear, stray lunch bags, scraps and crayons left behind.

Rich returned from driving as lightning flashed. The rain pelted down and we dashed for the house. Juggling toast and mugs of tea, Dave and I followed the others to the dining room. Each time the staff met, Rich, Bill and Ellie took side chairs, leaving Dave and me the ends of the oval table. Like parents.

"Well, we made it half way!" Dave grinned as he sat down. "Four weeks down and four to go—"

"Thanks to Gail," I said. "Today could have been the end." I told them about the note and Mrs. Sexton's reaction.

"I like mine better." Bill pulled a wrinkled paper from his T-shirt pocket. "Found it inside the guitar."

"Mine was taped to the easel—" Ellie withdrew a folded note from her jeans.

"I felt something scratchy in my swim trunks." Dave laughed, slapping his on the table.

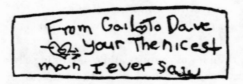

Rich grinned. "Gosh," he said, "and I thought I got the only one!"

We reviewed the week, talked bout the kids' behavior—how it related to issues the parents had discussed, and projected plans for the week ahead. Frankie's and Laura's return. Gail's impending hearing. Nathaniel's need for extra support. The message in his airplane game—how his attempts to keep his world in control always end in disaster.

"You've handled him well, Bill. Does he know you might be leaving?" Dave finally asked the question I'd avoided.

"It wouldn't be fair for me to go now, with his mother missing." Bill didn't look up from his notes.

"I'm glad you'll stay."

"It's only because of the kids."

From across the table, David looked at me and nodded, before he turned back to Billy. "Then I'm glad for the kids' sake. But for me as well. I've come to like our little team. Enough, in fact, to issue the ultimate challenge. I say we plan an overnight camp-out."

"Take these kids camping?" The old vitality was back in Billy's voice. "We'd have to be crazy!"

"That settles it then!" David thumped his fist on his notebook, "I know someone who'll lend us the tents."

20

Saturday noon, Ellen came running from the mailbox, waving a letter from Ann. I sat beside her on the wobbly wooden porch steps while we read it silently together.

Ann had decorated the top page with shooting stars and letters that looked three dimensional, like greeting cards she had made as a child.

> A camp at our house! What a wonderful idea! Any other summer I'd be right there too. But here I am sitting on a patch of dirt, surrounded by a circle of curious little bare-bottomed kids who've come with their families to buy food and clothes at the traveling market which circulates from village to village.
>
> It's taken almost six months to make it from Egypt to Tanzania by incredibly crowded rickety buses, and often on foot—or should I say on two swollen blistered feet?
>
> I want to stay and see more of this amazing continent as long as my money holds out. I've been able to stretch it this far by sleeping in mosques and missions along the way.
>
> I've met some fascinating people, watched a witch doctor cure a dying child, even attended an Arab wedding where the bride and her attendants wore crowns of lighted candles and made eerie haunting cries by clicking their tongues . . .

... although I miss you all, I feel as though there's something I have to work out by keeping on the move. Right now, for me, the thought of coming back either to work or to continue in school is both remote and painful. I can't imagine what I'd want or be ready to do ...

Ellie wiped away a tear. "It—it just doesn't sound like Ann ..."

Hard for me, too, to connect the uncertain writer with our capable, confident Ann. The older sister who'd cared for Ellen so tenderly, so often.

I felt choked up too.

"Look, Ellie," I pointed to the date. "She wrote this over a month ago. Maybe Ann's already changed her mind."

21

On Monday morning I poured some milk in my coffee and carried the mug out to the porch, wondering how much more time I'd have at this house. In spite of the camp, the agent had a bid from possible buyers. He wanted to contact my former husband at the writers' colony. I was glad the studios had no phones. Communicating by mail would delay the process.

I was waiting for Frankie, whose father had said he'd bring him early, on the way to work.

Sure enough, their big gray Buick rolled to a halt at our mailbox at exactly 8:25. Pudgy Frank, in crisp beige shorts and thick white knee socks, got out without protesting, though he barely acknowledged his father's wave. He stood in the road till the car was out of sight, then shuffled dejectedly through the gate. "Nice going, Frank." I got up from the wooden step. "You ought to be pleased with yourself. And I'm sure glad to see you."

The wrong approach, if there was a right one. The hefty baby-faced thirteen-year-old burst into screams, his face instantly sopping with tears and infantile drool.

"Mother! Mother!" He buried his face in his Popeye beach towel. "I want my mother!—I want her now!"

"I'd like to help you Frank." I stepped closer. He lashed at me with his towel.

"Stay away, bitch! I don't need you—I want my mother." A corner of the towel struck my leg.

Catching it, I decided I ought to change tactics. "Just how scared do you feel, Frank?"

"Huh?" He looked up, surprised. "Whaddaya mean by that?"

"I mean, like on a scale from one to ten, how high is your fear? A five? A seven?" I hoped that pausing to rate the feeling would distance him from its impact.

But he screamed back, "Eleven! Is that high enough for you, you witch? Eleven!"

"Too high." I shook my head. "Ten's the top, and no one stays at ten very long. Oh, and take your towel. It's for drying you, not for flapping at me."

"Oh no!" the burly boy sank to the dewy grass, his face in the orange towel. "I can't go in the water! I can't do it! Don't try to make me! And don't anyone call me baby!"

Skipper trudged by to Ellen's outstretched arms as Frank and I made a deal. He'd come to circle if he didn't have to swim. I agreed—for today.

But as the other kids gathered, Frankie eyed his old tree trunk, and tried to bolt.

"Easy, Frank." I gripped his hand. "You're going to be okay." The kids were singing when he doubled over, one hand on his heart, the other on his stomach. "Breathe deeply. Count to fifty. You'll feel better soon."

Frankie followed me around all day. He sat beside me while I tutored other children. Buried his head in his arms on the kitchen counter while the "cookers" squeezed fresh orange juice and concocted a raisin-nut dessert. Screamed through the wooden cabinet, "Are you there? Are you waiting?" when he had to use the toilet. After lunch I got a hit in the ball game and Frankie scurried after me as I made a dash to first base. The outfielders hooted and jeered, "Who's yer fat little shadow?"

His face contorted. "Leave me alone! Can't ya see I don't have my mother! Can't ya see I'm tryin'?"

As the week progressed the only activities he attended were those I went to with him. In art, Frankie molded a Play-Doh "mother kangaroo," with a baby in her pocket. He watched the puppet groups but when Bill tried to hand him one he let it drop to the ground.

It was difficult to spend so much time with one child, especially now, when Bill was needed by Nathaniel. With both of us less available, Adam wandered from group to group, talking to himself. "Spkakk! Thoom! This is the time for the Torch. Only his flaming body can absorb the impact . . . Okay then, Torchy, there's only one thing to do . . . burn a path through the eye of the torrent . . ."

More disturbingly, he'd pinch and scratch himself, clawing at his arms and shoulders.

Rodney began acting out again, fighting in ball games, pushing kids in the water, running through games the girls were playing, taking their jump rope away. He delighted in the tantrums he could evoke from Frankie by tapping his shoulder to get his attention, and when Frank turned around, pretending he was sucking on a baby bottle till Frank began to wail.

And Frankie's dependency on me caused trouble with Gail. "Don't bother 'bout me. Just stick with your baby," she'd say, then storm away. "Who care you like him best? I be goin' home."

She turned to Dave for attention. In the water Gail performed handstand after handstand, insisting he look only at her. If he turned away even for a minute she'd cry.

The uncertainty of her future was terrible for Gail and for her foster parents. It weighed on all of us.

Every day she and Maria played frenetic versions of the good mother–bad kid game.

Finally, Thursday, a letter came to me at the clinic.

Re: Brown, Gail

Dear Ms. Craig:
    This is to inform you that the hearing on the Termination of Parental Rights concerning Gail Marie Brown is scheduled for Monday, August 8 at 10 A.M. Your testimony in this matter is vital.

Very truly yours,
Saul Helpern
Attorney General

I phoned Bertha Lapin, Gail's Protective Service worker. "Will I have to testify?"

"You may never be called on, but be prepared. Review her record. You might be asked how well she's adjusted at the Bennetts'."

How well Gail adjusted. It took an hour to review her bulky folder, beginning with the state's first contact.

> . . . one of six children born to Lillian Brown, an alcoholic who disappears for periodic bouts of drinking. At these times Gail stays home from school, assuming full responsibility for younger siblings. At nine she is also employed outside the home caring for an elderly bedridden woman in the building, who pays her five dollars weekly for helping her in and out of bed, doing dishes and cleaning a two-room apartment. The child spends her money on food for her siblings . . .

There was one report after another of suspected neglect. Investigations by Protective Service. The judge's decision to postpone removal of the children on the mother's promise to attend A.A., which she never did. A hearing six months later, which Gail's mother failed to attend. The two-year-old boy found wandering in the street. A younger baby hospitalized for malnutrition. Court action to remove the other children, including Gail.

A psychiatrist's evaluation:

> . . . the child alternates between episodes of tearfulness and forced good humor . . . not a disturbed girl, but a child in crisis. . . . In answer to what she'd like if she had three wishes, the girl replied, "a whole family with a mother and father," and "to be somebody." She couldn't think of a third wish . . .

The psychologist's report:

> Current testing indicates a child functioning within the Low Average to Borderline Defective range on the psycho-

metric. Other test data suggest her basic equipment is intact and that the lag in cognitive development and the depressed level of functioning are reactive to her life experiences and the current developmental problems with which she is confronted . . .

A letter from Gail's former teacher:

. . . I will miss her. She's had difficulty academically, but Gail has coped with overwhelming responsibility in the home. I enclose a language paper she did in class. It describes more clearly than I can the kind of life she's led.

Gail B.   May 2
                              Languge—T.V.
1.   it make us hungry to see T.V.
     like when you dont got no food and show food on
     T.V. and you wish you had some.
     like your walking down street and see boy eating
     somthing and want to go to boy and snatch it outta
     him hand.
2.   T.V. make us think winter.
     like when snow come down and it cold
     and when people got them mittens an got boots and
     we is cold.
3.   make think of night time
     when you in bed some one be crying so you get bad
     dreams.

22

On August eighth at 9:45 A.M. I walked toward the court house wondering what would become of Gail. Then I saw her through the window that framed the three-tiered stairway. She stood on the landing,
her hands and nose flat against the glass, staring at the half-filled
parking lot. I waved. She disappeared.

Both doors swung open as I climbed the bank of stairs. It was the
first time I'd seen her in a dress—soft rosy nylon, puffed sleeves, lacy
collar, wide sash tied in back, streamers to the hemline. She wore
pink socks and white buckled shoes. Tiny pink bows were tied to
each of her many little braids. "Gail," I said, "you're beautiful!"

She didn't respond to the compliment. "You seen my mother?"
She glanced at all the cars, then ran down the steps, across the
blacktop, up and down the sidewalk, left and right. Back to me. "You
got any gum? Any candy?"

I found a half roll of forgotten Lifesavers in the bottom of my
purse. Gail stuffed them all in her mouth.

"Bennetts here?" I asked.

"Waiting room," she drooled, pointing up the stairway.

"How about Miss Lapin?"

"In there." The candy was packed in her cheeks, causing her to
drool when she answered.

"I'll tell her I'm here. Want to come?" I put out my hand.

"Uh-uh." Gail scampered up the stairs. "I'm watchin'. For my mother. I'm gonna count to a hundred, but if she ain't here by then I—I'll hafta start all over."

The office of Protective Service occupied a warehouse-sized room—the whole ground floor of the building. Opening the door, I felt a rush, a sudden assault of energy. Voices, ringing phones; there were row after row of desks—some sixty in all. The men and women were writing, talking into phones, interviewing anxious-looking people, searching battered files.

I finally spotted Bertha, her wavy dark hair cut shorter, standing in a sleeveless violet maternity dress, the color of her large round eyes. She held the telephone receiver between her ear and shoulder and scribbled me a message: "Thanks for coming. Got two emergencies on hold. I'll be up when Gail gets called. Maybe coffee after?"

I found Gail working her way along the first row of desks, begging for food. A shirt-sleeved man obliged her with Saran-Wrapped cookies from his lunch bag. A thin blonde extended a stick of gum, without interrupting her talk on the phone.

"Hey, c'mon dear," I said, taking Gail's hand. "I think you're nervous, not hungry."

I exchanged pleasantries with the Bennetts, who were sitting stiffly on long wooden benches in the waiting room. I did another quick review of Gail's record while she ran up and down the stairs, paused by me and then the Bennetts, peeking into the courtroom every time the door swung open. She approached everyone who went in or came out to ask for food, even the armed policeman.

A short, fat red-headed man in a cocoa-brown suit the color of his freckles beckoned to me and ushered us into his closet-sized office. He was Gail's court-appointed advocate. What did I plan to say, he asked, closing the door.

How could I testify against her mother? I'd never even met her. Nor had I access to the Bennetts' house or their daily lives with Gail. I could only describe what I knew—Gail's ability, her behavior, her craving for affection and yet her avoidance of closeness. My certainty that she had to be rescued from limbo and never bounced around again. Stability and continuity of care were what Gail—and every child—needed.

Gail's mother still hadn't arrived. Our appearance was postponed until the afternoon session. "If she isn't here by two the judge will go ahead."

Mr. Bennett looked at the clock, protesting. "The woman's known for months. It just isn't fair to give her more time now."

He and his wife decided to take a walk and Gail accompanied me to a diner several blocks from the courthouse.

Encouraged by the judge's delay, she skipped along beside me, clutching a brown paper bag with the tattered nightgown she had originally brought from home.

"It's the only thing I'll be takin' back, 'ceptin' for the doll I got for Christmas. I'm givin' that to Ina Claire, my sister. God," she chattered, "I remember the first night I got tooken to the Bennetts'— man, that place looked so-o-o-o gigantic! I wasn't afraid of them new people or the great big bed I hadda sleep in all alone. Only the dog. I swear, that dog look like a monster! Hey!" She stopped in front of a liquor store. "C'n I have a dollar? You wouldn't believe how glad my mother be if I get her some wine—"

"Uh-uh Gail, no wine. But you can have a dollar to spend in that place on the corner."

I waited in front of the variety store until Gail came out clutching cigarettes and a blue plastic long-stemmed rose.

She arranged the gifts on her paper placemat at the table, and talked as she bounced on the padded bench. "What if my mother lives in a dump? You ain't never gonna visit me, right? What if my sister wets the bed again? My mother say she gonna lock her up in the closet." She continued to fidget on the bench.

"Some a the other kids, they got a different 'plexion. They lighter and she don't hit them so much."

It was hard for me to accept, a black parent favoring the lighter-skinned children. Yet I'd heard it before.

"Gail"—I reached across the table for her hand, hoping to settle her down—"your memories don't sound like happy ones."

"I wonder where them social workers put them? What if one a the kids got left outside on the road? Maybe some a them still get to see our mama. If I didn't live with the Bennetts, I could go back to her, too."

"No, Gail. Don't blame the Bennetts."

hope of retaining custody of your daughter, you must get yourself a sponsor and faithfully attend the A.A. meetings. We'll reconvene in this courtroom in exactly three months for the final determination."

The Bennetts escorted Gail down the stairs. She moved like a robot till they got outside. There she left them standing in the shadow of the building, broke away and threw herself against her mother's rigid body. "Mama, Mama, do what the judge man said! Mama, please, so we can all come home."

"I don't live there any more," her mother said, pulling away. "My life is different now."

The man in the car gunned the motor till it roared and backfired. "You comin' or not?" he snarled at the woman.

Gail looked dazed as the car sped into the street. "Everything bad is coming true. Everything."

I started toward her, but backed away to let the Bennetts, arms outstretched, faces pained, deal with the stricken girl. The moment they touched her, Gail began to kick and scream.

"Leave me alone! I hate you both! And I hate that fuckin' judge and I hate the whole damn world including God—"

Gail was still yelling and struggling in the front seat between her foster parents as they drove away.

"Most kids like Gail, who've been in foster care for over a year, never do go back home." Bertha paused to sip her coffee at the counter of the diner. For her this was also lunch, at three P.M.

"Why can't the money go to keeping families together?" I felt so frustrated. "At least we ought to try."

"Hey, you know as well as I do the farther the child is moved from home the more the state will spend. Fifteen thousand dollars a year for kids in residential treatment! But not one extra cent to strengthen multiproblem families, or understand their needs. And if we workers think it's safe to delay, and God forbid a kid we're responsible for gets hurt or killed, we're the ones who get attacked. Sometimes I go to bed at night praying it won't be one of the kids in my caseload who dies.

"And there's the rub. Why we get so many inexperienced workers. Most of us burn out in a couple of years. I tell you, I had trouble listening to all the rhetoric about the International Year of the Child! If our society cared about kids, would people like me—who try to save their lives—be earning thirteen thousand dollars a year? I've had it!" She shook her head. "No more doomed kids for me. I'll be happy to be staying home, taking care of Oscar." She patted her swollen stomach.

Driving back, I still felt puzzled. If Gail's mother really wanted her, she knew she had to join A.A. She didn't. So why had she come to court?

23

Laura's father parked near the barn. He withdrew a folding wheel-chair from the car trunk, locked it into position and lifted a thin limp figure, right leg in a rigid cast, from the passenger seat to the wheel-chair.

Dave, Bill, Ellie and I gathered to meet Laura. She received our hugs like a rag doll. She was pale and so thin that the wheelchair seemed to engulf her. Orange barrettes held Laura's sand-colored hair in two wispy pigtails. I was pleased to see her wearing her navy blue Camp Hopewell T-shirt.

The cast was much autographed and kept her right leg stiffly extended beyond the footrest of the wheelchair. Her father gently draped a lacy cream-colored shawl over her lap, arranging it to cover her toes.

He returned from the car with her crutches, urging Laura to "let these good people help you," and bent to kiss her goodbye.

"I can't," she said, turning away.

The other children arrived one by one, spotted Laura, and re-treated to safe positions. Skipper pawed at Ellen. She picked him up. Tim clutched Camp Dog's flea collar, dragging her under an obscure bush to assess the situation. Adam, towel around his neck, flew down the driveway, stopped abruptly and reversed direction, looking over his shoulder every few leaps to flash wary glances and finger hex signs at the stark wheelchair and its lifeless-looking occupant.

"I'll get Adam." Bill left the little group surrounding Laura.

Although we'd kept the children informed about Laura's surgery and her release from the hospital, I'd overheard Gail bet Carlos that Laura would return "without any legs." And Rodney spread a rumor that she had died, protesting "no one here can take a joke" when Ellen found Maria crying. Seeing Laura in her wheelchair must have seemed like seeing a ghost.

Tree by tree Frankie worked his way from his father's car to the maple tree behind me. "Pssst—" he beckoned urgently. "How come she can't walk?"

"I think she can." I left Laura with Dave. "It's a matter of really trying."

"When she takes off her clothes"—Frankie clutched the crotch of his jeans—"will she still be a girl?"

"Of course, dear, just like you'll always be a male, Laura will always be—"

"My mother got glass in her foot," he interrupted. "I'm not sure if it ever came out." Leaning against the tree, he slid on his spine till his bottom hit the gnarled surface roots. "I wanna go home," he whimpered. "My stomach's coming up."

I sat down beside him, my hand on his shoulder. "You can keep it down, Frank. It's part of that old scared feeling isn't it? It's hard for me, too, seeing Laura in a wheelchair. And I think the idea of people being hurt makes you feel afraid. Is that right?"

". . . not the only thing." I had to lean closer to hear him. "Other stuff too. Like bridges falling down and airplanes crashing and elevators getting stuck and spiders and noises like trains and the dark when my mother dries her hair in the bathroom."

"Dries her hair?"

"If the blower got wet she could be electrocuted."

"But I'm sure she's careful."

So many fears. Those who had taught Frankie to see the world as a scary place had done a convincing job.

I wondered what would happen to him in his late teens and early twenties, those trying years when so many youngsters on the verge of independence suffer from emotional problems and when some tragically see no alternative but suicide.

Could Frankie sustain himself without depending on his parents?

Or was he already too damaged by their double binding, their hollow words betrayed by their own behavior:

- You need me/I resent your dependence.
- You are my little treasure/You are a goddamn nuisance.
- There's nothing to be afraid of/The world is a scary place.

Would these confusing messages paralyze Frankie in his young adulthood? I hoped when camp was over I could continue to see him, to help him face his fear of leaving home.

I used to be put off by advocates of behavior modification, their talk of "positive and negative reinforcement," "modeling" and so on, and I was angry at seeing candy popped into the mouths of unsuspecting autistic children. Surely I treated my dog with more respect and humanity.

But I'd come to experience the joy of having children's behavior change rapidly through behavioral techniques. For many children I found behavior modification superior to the more introspective kinds of psychotherapy.

Frankie's fear of leaving his mother was displaced onto "mean classmates" and "teachers who yell." Desensitizing him to his panic by separating him from her for gradually longer periods of time and by exposing him to situations arousing less anxiety, then moving him gradually into more challenging activities, using relaxation exercises, might relieve his symptoms faster than months of probing talk-therapy sessions.

Exploration of the deep-seated reasons for his fears could begin after Frankie experienced success. Not while he was in crisis.

For now, I told him that chances of the things he worried about happening to him were slim. But I understood his feeling.

We did breathing exercises, tightening and relaxing of muscles. Frankie closed his eyes and squeezed his fist.

"Tighter. Tighter. Good. Now let go. Remember that when you're tense you can send your brain a message through your body . . . to relax . . ."

Frankie ran off to look at Laura's wheelchair.

Rich drove in late. Nathaniel, Rodney and the Hernandez children spilled from his car.

"We waited all that time for Gail," Carlos explained to Billy. "Rich thought she'd be comin', 'cause the judge decided not to do nothin'."

Maria noticed Laura. "You come back! Hooray!" But Laura pulled the shawl up over head when Maria ran to hug her. The tiny girl, dark eyes wide and puzzled, stopped and backed away.

Nathaniel held his snake jar in front of Laura's covered face. "Remember me?" he affected a squealy voice. "My name's Killer. You think I growed since you seen me?"

Laura neither moved nor answered.

Both Killer and Nathaniel stuck out their tongues.

Dave wheeled Laura to opening circle. Bill said it was good to see her. From the children's wary glances and gloomy faces, his was a minority opinion. Only Rodney appeared unaffected. He alone felt "dy-no-mite" in answer to the morning question, and was swiveling his hips like a hula dancer when the Bennetts' car screeched to a halt at the gate. Gail banged the door and sauntered down the driveway, head high, chest out, bottom wriggling defiantly.

"Here comes Gail." Carlos pointed.

Here comes trouble, I thought, waving to the Bennetts. They sped away without acknowledging my greeting.

"You late, girl." Rodney looked pleased to see her.

"Ain't none of your beeswax," she snarled.

"Oh, a wise ass! First she come late," he said, pointing with his thumb, "then she come full a hate."

"Shut up, you Mr. think-you-so-Big Man. You the wise ass! Actin' big—like a father—when you ain't even got one."

I caught her. "That's it Gail. Rodney's here, like the rest of us, dealing with his problems. It isn't fair to be cruel, even if you don't feel happy."

"Who ain't happy?" She wrenched her hand from mine. "Why I wouldn't be happy?"

"Because your mother—" Maria began.

"You think I mind about her?" Gail seized a fistful of Maria's T-shirt, yanking the trembling girl to her feet. Carlos pounced on Gail. José leaped to protect Maria.

Rich grabbed Carlos. I caught Gail in a tight hug intended both to comfort and restrain her.

We held another group discussion. Rodney piously suggested what he'd so often been told. "She oughtta say it in words, 'stead of wiping all her sweat on us."

Gail crossed her arms and legs and turned away. "Why should I? I don't trust nobody here and nothin' nobody says. And I don't care 'bout her—" she spat, "the one that useta be my mother."

"I believe you do," Tim murmured.

But Gail retreated into stony silence.

Later, she drew the last in her series of houses. This one had no flowers, heavy smoke from the chimney, and the windows seemed to be weeping.

It was Dave's turn to lead the closing circle. "What would you choose, if you could be whatever you wanted?"

"I'd be a marriage-wrecker," Tim said, sitting hunched, knees against his chest. " 'cause anyway I already am one."

"You think you wrecked a marriage?" Dave pursued Tim's answer. My eye caught the lineup of adults outside the fence. Skipper's mother always came early, to watch her son. Today she was joined by three men—Frankie's father, Laura's father, and Mr. Bennett.

"I'd rather be a baby," Frankie drooled. "Then I'd get to stay home."

Laura took her turn. "I'd be a big old oak tree." She looked up at the oversized branches, then slumped down in her wheelchair.

"How come?" Rich smiled.

" 'Cause oak trees stand up straight and they can live forever."

"Uh-uh!" Gail shook her head. "They could chop you down."

When circle ended, Gail ignored her foster father, although he called her, and dashed into Richie's car.

"Mrs. Craig," his voice demanded, but his dark eyes pleaded, "my wife and I need to talk to you. We want Gail to hear it."

Gail was crouching under Rodney's legs. I had to insist before she'd get out. Mr. Bennett went to get his wife, still in the front seat of their Volkswagen, staring straight ahead. He had to help her out. I was shocked by her condition.

She was limping and had buttons missing on her blouse. An elastic bandage was strapped around her leg and there was an ugly purple bruise on her cheekbone. Hairpins dangled from her bun.

"Mrs. Bennett, what happened?" I held the gate.

"Gail didn't tell you?" Her husband, on whom she was leaning, looked around the yard. "Gail, come here! I want you to listen."

Gail stepped out from behind a tree, head hanging, and shuffled toward us.

I led them across the porch through the living room, into the dining room, Gail following warily, keeping distant, watching at the doorway as Mrs. Bennett moaned into a chair. Then Gail scurried to a seat next to mine, across the table from her foster parents.

"It's hard to begin." His voice was soft and husky. "We're both so discouraged . . ."

"Discouraged!" his wife interrupted, trembling.

Gail edged her chair so close to mine the wooden seats were scraping.

The woman held a yellow tissue to her bruise. "Bert, I'm more than discouraged." She sounded angry and wounded. "I've had it! Gail doesn't want to be with us. If her mother doesn't get her, the state will have to look for some other place—I can't do any more."

"Good!" Gail spat, leaning toward the woman. "Why doncha send me to Long Meadow, like my mother!"

Long Meadow was a "correctional center" for troubled and troublesome girls. I realized that in spite of the hearing Gail would still identify with her mother for a long time.

"You're not going to force me to do that." Mr. Bennett shook his finger at Gail.

The room was electric with emotion. His burning eyes held Gail's narrowed, angry glare. Then he began to toy with his bristly black beard, and slowly told the story:

He'd left for work at seven this morning. His wife made scrambled eggs for Gail.

She said her real mother's food was better. Mrs. Bennett asked her to eat. Gail threw the plate and eggs in the sink. Mrs. Bennett got so angry she slapped her. Gail ran around the house, screaming for her mother. Mrs. Bennett wanted to apologize. She tried to hug her. Gail went wild. Cursing, kicking, screaming, punching.

In hysterics, the woman had called her husband. They dropped Gail here at camp and drove to their family physician. He'd treated her bruises and contusions, but he was deeply concerned. Mrs. Bennett's blood pressure had zoomed sky high.

He'd been an advocate for battered children, but this, the doctor warned Mr. Bennett, this was a case of *parent* abuse. If his wife was at risk, the child should go.

I felt Gail's body shudder, heard her quick intake of breath, but when I reached for her hand she yanked it away.

Mr. Bennett glanced helplessly from his wife to Gail, whose lips were sealed in defiance.

He shook his head, then studied his hands, breathing hard before he spoke. "Gail's doing exactly what I did as a kid, and I wish she wouldn't repeat it. I made myself unwelcome in every foster home I went to. Eight of them. Some I liked. Some I hated. It didn't matter. I threw rocks at the windows, set shrubbery on fire.

"I didn't know it then"—he finally looked at Gail—"but I was afraid if I got close, the people would abandon me—like my mother. So I—I acted like I didn't care. Turned on them first before they got the chance to do it to me. Gail, honey"—his voice choked—"don't do this to yourself. Or to us. I know how you feel, but let us care for you. We won't let you down." He stretched his hand across the table but Gail shrank away.

"No Bert." His wife clasped his arm. "Don't beg her. I couldn't go through this again. Let her go. I just can't handle that child." She rubbed her bandaged leg. "I thought—I thought she'd help us get over Effie, but she hasn't."

Gail began to hum and tap her feet.

I knew this should have been dealt with before, their reason for becoming foster parents. A traumatized child can't replace a dead one, not yet fully mourned, idealized in the head and mind of her mother. Such foster placement is doomed from the beginning.

Mrs. Bennett was crying. Her husband patted her back. "We can't replace our daughter, dear."

Gail tapped harder. Arms crossed, she looked at the ceiling, humming louder. I put my hand on her jiggly knees.

"Gail's not like Effie, dear. But Effie wasn't perfect either. And dying doesn't make anyone perfect. Let's remember all we knew about her. I'm sure she would have worried us too, in different ways than Gail. And we never never would have dreamed of saying she had to leave us."

I wanted to leap across the table, hold up his hand and cheer for him. I had seen it happen so often, foster kids being rejected, shunted to yet another home, another set of strangers, labeled "unworkable" by unprepared and disillusioned foster parents.

Mr. Bennett cupped his hand over his wife's as she blotted the tears coursing down her cheeks. Gail, still humming, continued to survey the dining room's cracked ceiling.

The grandfather clock chimed four-fifteen. I'd be late getting to the clinic. We had to resolve the impasse with deference to Mrs. Bennett's health and feelings, but I knew they mustn't abandon Gail.

Not sure of where it would lead, I tried to summarize the situation. The tragic loss of their daughter. Gail's arrival from her very different life style. Her gradually improved behavior. The trauma for them all—in court—only the day before. Gail, who couldn't show her feelings to her mother, venting the hurt and rage on Mrs. Bennett this morning.

All the emotions so raw, so intense now. No time to make a major decision. If Gail would agree to try to talk things out with them, as she'd begun to do at camp . . . if they would postpone deciding, Barry at the clinic was starting a group specifically for foster parents, and they could be included.

Mrs. Bennett glanced cautiously at her husband, then lowered her eyes to the tissue she was twisting and tearing.

"I think"—Mr. Bennet looked at her, at Gail, at me—"I believe we're willing to try, if Gail is. You know, honey"—he smiled at her and nodded—"I'd like to think about adoption."

Gail brushed my hair back and cupped her hands to my ears. "Why they gotta do it legal?" she whispered. "He wanna be my father; well, tell him he ain't!"

"Uh-uh." I drew myself away. "No fair keeping secrets now, Gail, when everyone's trying to talk."

"Why you gotta do it legal?" she demanded, censoring her other comment.

"We're a long way from that," Mrs. Bennett said, finally looking at Gail. "But," she got up and limped around the table, "I'm willing to try it a week at a time if—if you are."

Gail pushed her chair back slowly. Her head was down as she shuffled toward the anxious woman. I couldn't see her eyes and I worried about her intentions. The two were a yard apart when Gail stopped moving. Her body tilted forward toward Mrs. Bennett, who gently pulled her closer.

Gail allowed herself to be hugged, but her own arms hung straight at her sides.

Mr. Bennett watched a minute before he got up and held his wife and their foster daughter.

Racing down Route One to the clinic, I smiled, wondering how often my mother might have entertained the thought of divorcing me. And I, my children. And they me, as a parent.

24

"Bertha Lapin's in her office," the receptionist said, handing me a stack of memos, "waiting for you to call her."

". . . I'll be leaving Friday," Bertha said, "Doctor's orders. So I tracked down Gail's mother for one last time this morning. Thought you'd like the answer to your question. Apparently her boyfriend's mother accused her of not really caring that her kids were taken. So she came to court to show her that she's not a lousy mother."

"Good old maternal instinct." My throat felt tight.

"She said it doesn't matter now. She's going to have another baby. So she signed the termination papers—on all the kids. She won't go back to court. Oh, thought you'd be interested—Judge Russell didn't recognize her, but she remembered him as the one who sent her to Long Meadow when she was eleven, almost the same age as Gail."

"Oh God, Bertha! Round and round it goes. Well, tell me, how do you think she really feels about losing Gail?"

"She said that Gail was always asking for something, and she could see she hasn't changed. Since we took away her kids, now we can keep them. Will you break it to Gail that there won't be another hearing? God knows when she'll be assigned a worker. There's no funding at all for my replacement."

"Ouch. That hurts! Okay, I'll tell her, but it won't be easy. I think it would help if she could see her brothers and sisters soon. They haven't been together since Gail went to the Bennetts'. Before you leave, would you arrange a reunion?"

"No way! From now till Friday I'm full time on emergencies only. But I'll send you the list. They're all in different communities, so they all have different workers. That's why they haven't met yet. Sorry I can't do it. I wish I had more time."

"I understand. Good luck to you, Bertha. Good luck with baby Oscar."

In my office later, I shuffled through papers, too tired to answer requests for summaries on our camp kids to help in planning fall school programs. Then on the bottom of the stack, I came to Barry's announcement:

ATTN–ALL STAFF:
Possibility of one year's funding for a pilot program. Outpatient Day Treatment designed for youngsters who might otherwise require hospitalization.
Goal: to allow children to remain in the community while doing extensive treatment with families.
Staff needs:
• Program Director
• Two full-time aides
Time is tight. Anyone interested should contact me right away.

Suddenly I felt wide awake. A brand new program. Intensive work with families. An exciting challenge. I picked up the phone to contact Barry but hung up halfway through dialing.

Why was I rushing into such a demanding program? To get swallowed up by others' problems? A chance to avoid my own?

Something warned me: Think it over. Discuss it first with Ceil, with my children. I wrote a noncommittal note to Barry: "May be interested in Day Treatment. Please call me at home. Eleanor" and left it in his mailbox.

• • •

Saturday morning Richard got his letter from the Peace Corps. A teaching assignment in Korea. Yellow forms for the dentist. Blue ones for the doctor. A list of immunizations. In three weeks, the group of volunteers would meet in San Francisco. Then a month of intensive training in Seoul, Korea. Instructions to call Washington, D.C., within forty-eight hours if his answer was affirmative. Airline tickets to follow.

He read it to us, to Bill, Ellie and me, in the kitchen. He talked excitedly while Ellen broiled English muffins and placed them around the platter full of scrambled eggs. For the first time in years we four sat together for breakfast.

Richard was full of plans and questions. Would I try to keep his convertible in running condition? Did we think he ought to sell his drums? There wasn't any question about it. Richard would be going to Korea.

Billy reached across the table and shook his brother's hand. Then he began to tell his own plans. He would go back to Boston to share a place with Nicola. She'd continue painting. He'd work on video taping. They'd both go to school. It was a statement. He wasn't asking my opinion. I'd have been hard-pressed to give it. Such freedom was never an option I could have considered at his age.

Ellie would rent a house with a group of fine arts students from her college rather than return to the dorm. "And what will you be doing, Mom? What are your plans?"

I explained about Day Treatment, and asked for their opinions. Rich knew I got a sense of renewal from pilot progams. Ellie thought the timing was perfect. Bill said I'd get new input for writing . . .

"Actually Ma"—Bill began to clear the table—"I think you oughtta write about us. This summer, I mean. But really tell it. Don't try to present us ideally. Wouldn't want you to suppress our personalities . . ."

Ellie took her easel out to the yard. I watched her from the kitchen window as she began to paint a picture of the barn. Millie Camp Dog wandered across the grass and stretched out under her easel.

Bill helped Rich drag his cymbals and drums down the driveway. At noon their friends arrived for a raucous jam. I held my breath when I saw our neighbor striding toward them, intent, perhaps, on complaining about the music.

But he'd been sent by his wife to hire them all to play at a party they'd be giving the following weekend. Laughing, I went upstairs to try to organize my closet. No point in moving things I had no use for.

25

We spent the seventh week preparing for the camp-out.

The activity committee voted Tim their chairman after he put his own name into nomination. His platform was his promise to research "authentic Indian activities." Diane held her stomach and said she was too sick to vote. Tim counted Adam's hex signs as his first endorsement, his own raised hand as the second and when Skipper tried to mimic Adam's flying fingers Tim announced he'd won a unanimous decision and delegated Ellen to help Adam and Skipper mold a peace pipe.

The menu committee was less cooperative, refusing Tim's demand to pound shucked corn into meal with stones, even when he brought in his encyclopedia with the pictures.

Frankie and José elected Nathaniel head of the Equipment Committee. Rich took them all except Frank, who wouldn't get into his car, to the hardware store to buy a rope for the tug of war, then to the home of the Boy Scout leader who had agreed to lend us tents.

By Tuesday, as excitement mounted, so did an underlying tension. The idea of sleeping out, even in a well-patrolled state park, generated fear.

"Will you bring a gun?" Carlos and José took turns asking Billy, Rich and David this question, "case something bad goes wrong."

"I forgot to tell you Killer's partly cobra," Nathaniel announced at closing circle. "You oughtta be glad havin' someone like him on the camp-out."

Maria told me secretly her brothers prayed for rain. "... they think they'll hate to go camping. But I know I'll like it. I'm askin' Holy Mary to make it sun."

Frankie swung from attending planning meetings with his committee to curling up on the lawn sobbing, "I can't do it! I can't go without my mother!"

"I'll help you, Frank."

"You're not helpin' me!" His kick missed my ankle. "You're only helpin' yourself! You just want perfect attendance!"

"Why you gotta be so hardheaded, boy?" Rodney strutted over. "Just make like we all be you mother."

"Get outta here! Leave me alone! You're crazy too! Maaa-oh-Maaa, come get me!"

That day Rodney used the bathroom after Frankie and stormed out, complaining that the toilet was completely plugged. The rental company, too, had been finding wads of paper and threatened to end our contract for service, so we had all been watching for the culprit. But Rodney's condemnation of Frankie was inconclusive, since he himself was a suspect. His challenge to Frank, "you better admit what you done there or you won't be going nowhere," was neither proof of his own innocence nor any threat to Frankie.

The food committee, headed by Carlos, argued over menus from Monday until Thursday, the day we all went shopping.

"Who don't like tacos?" José, following his brother's instructions, conducted an opinion poll by grabbing hold of T-shirts and barking into each face, "Do YOU like tacos?" Everyone did, except for Rodney, who held out for hot dogs.

In the checkout line at the supermarket Rodney dropped a package of hot-dog rolls into Carlos' shopping cart. His comment, "People rather have tacos insteada real bread, they oughta be livin' in Spicland instead—" could have provoked a major battle. But at that moment Gail rolled Laura's wheelchair through the emergency exit, triggering the sirens that summoned three police cars.

—— 26 ——

There was no camp Friday. We used the day to get ourselves prepared and round up extra sleeping bags for kids who didn't have
them. The children began arriving at three P.M., loaded down with
bed rolls, cooking gear, paper bags with pajamas. But Frankie wasn't
among them.

Ellie took the phone call. "His mother says he feels nauseous."

"Don't hang up, El—" I tore across the porch to the kitchen
phone and insisted on speaking to Frank. I got, instead, his mother's
dull refusal. "My son is ill. I already told your daughter." Click.

Wild with fury, I was searching through my notebook for
Frankie's father's office number when our telephone rang again.

"Hello?" A tiny voice. "I think I wanna go."

"Good boy, Frank. We'll wait till you get here."

"Can't," he whispered. "My mother swore when I tole her I was
better. Now she says the car's not workin'."

"I'll be there soon."

Dave took off with Laura beside him, her wheelchair in the trunk
of his car under mounds of sleeping bags. Diane, Maria, and Tim—
his arms around Camp Dog—all sat in the back.

Rodney helped Rich strap the khaki tent bags onto the ski rack on
top of his convertible while Carlos, José, and Gail, hugging Ellen,
piled in.

Bill and I loaded the kerosene stove, lanterns, and two Styrofoam containers crammed with milk, eggs, ground meat and cheeses into the back of the station wagon Ceil Black had lent us. We put Adam and Nathaniel in the middle seat, and headed for Hidden Valley Terrace to pick up Frankie.

"Ya never know!" Bill whistled, turning down the road. We could see Frank from the corner, an overgrown, overweight kid in red plaid knee pants and floppy white beach hat, standing in the middle of the road, flagging us down with a folded road map.

Ignoring his pale-faced mother at the window, Frank got in the car beside me. Billy honked, I waved, as we turned around in her driveway. But she continued to stare.

Frankie unfolded his road map. "It's really my father's, but I borrowed it so I could find out where I'm going. I never knew that before."

"I'm with you, kid." Billy glanced at Frank and smiled.

We drove thirty minutes to Rocky Hill Park. Nathaniel held Killer's jar to the window. "He never seen no kinda woods." Adam flew his super-hero doll with the Kleenex cape all around the back seat, occasionally crashing into the ceiling or the overhead light. "Thok! K-k-k-pow!"

Frankie, beside me, finger-traced our route on the road map. Bill drove and hummed. I felt content until Nathaniel broke the mood. "Take this street, Bill!" he screamed. "Please, Bill, please, you gotta!" Nathaniel drummed his fist on Billy's shoulder.

Billy responded, turning right into a street lined with three-decker tenement houses with sagging porches.

"I think it's where my momma's at! Her boyfriend, he live on a street like this—in—in a old brown house." Nathaniel's head swiveled left and right. A gray house, many peeling once-white houses. No big brown one. "Go left, Bill! No, I mean right! Go right again! Down here. They brung me down a road like this one."

Billy looked at me. Shall we?

Might as well, I nodded.

"No. This ain't it. Maybe it's the next street! I mean that one."

"Nat," I said, "a lot of neighborhoods look alike."

"Uh-uh." He didn't have an address.

"Sorry, kid," Billy said kindly, heading down the dead end street to turn around.

"We're lost!" Frankie whined, curling up on the floor in back. "Lost! Lost! I knew it. I knew we'd get lost!"

"No we're not, Frank."

"We're lost! I can't swallow!" Drool dribbled down his chin, onto his Camp Hopewell T-shirt. "If I ever see my mother again I'm gonna tell her! She'll put you both in jail. Maaaaa! Ohhhh . . . we're lost . . ."

"Thok! Varoom! These fools should never have heeded that luckless lad. We're now but sitting ducks. F-zak! I must don my wonder gloves." Adam donned the invisible gloves. "Guide this fantasy flight to maximum maneuverability. Zok! Varo-o-om!"

"They here! They didn't have no accident!"

Carlos zigzagged through the trees to greet us. Frankie whined and clung to my shirttail while I unloaded the car. Nathaniel and Carlos toted the Styrofoam food boxes, the stove and lanterns to our campsite. Bill and I followed, leading Frankie and Nathaniel along the path, which was crunchy with pine needles and scented with their freshness.

On the winding road from the entrance to the park we'd driven past clusters of tents and trailers. For their sakes and ours I hoped we wouldn't have neighbors. Dave must have had the same idea, because we had a choice location, private, and right on the lake with our own dock and the use of two canoes and a rowboat.

Teams of kids led by Dave, Rich and Ellen put up the ten khaki tents in two rows between the woods and the water on a long flat meadow of velvety grass, on either side of the mammoth stone fireplace.

Laura, in her wheelchair, held a lapful of wooden stakes and handed one at a time to Gail, who distributed them to José and Rodney, the hammerers. Carlos, Dave and Maria adjusted center poles. Ellie helped Diane tie up the canvas flaps that created doors and windows.

Bill and I enlisted Nathaniel, Adam and Frankie to help us organize the food and store it all on one of the three long picnic tables on the far side of the fireplace. I enjoyed seeing Adam follow directions and Frankie forget himself to snoop through shopping bags muttering, "Cookies, cookies, where are you, cookies?"

When all ten tents were secured, the kids began racing around trying to decide who'd "live" where. Gail and Maria quickly established that tents on the left were "the girls' side." But arguments flared over who'd get the one closest to the lake.

Rodney strolled away from the discussion, tossed his sleeping bag into the tent everyone wanted, and stood in the doorway, arms folded, blocking the entrance. "No sense comin' near, 'cause Big Man livin' here."

Nathaniel, Carlos, José, Gail, Maria, eyeing Rodney nervously, called a secret huddle to plan their counter strategy, while Adam, wandering aimlessly, ventured too close to Rodney's newly-claimed turf.

"I say Big Man live here, so beat it, you queer."

It looked as though I would have to assign the tents equitably. Rich and Ellie helped me number slips of paper for a lottery and put them into Frankie's cotton beach hat, which he volunteered as a container.

Dave blew the shrill whistle dangling from the leather cord around his neck and we formed a circle for the drawing. Rodney left the tent reluctantly.

Tim had brought his own one-man pup tent, insisting he wanted to sleep alone. He passed the hat, "since I'm the only one present with no interest in the outcome of this contest," and each person chose a slip of paper.

Rodney drew first and leapt up for a victory dance. As luck would have it, he'd managed to draw number one, and reclaimed the tent closest to the lake. Nathaniel got number two and chose to be Rodney's roommate, though Rodney protested that Killer made three so Nathaniel and Killer ought to sleep elsewhere.

José got the third choice and begged to sleep with his brother, which would work out well. Bill could be with Adam and Richard with Frankie. That afforded Dave the fifth tent on the "boys' side" to himself.

Gail and Maria chose "tent one" on the "girls' side," opposite Rodney and Nathaniel. Laura and Ellen would be next to them. Diane asked to sleep alone and there were enough tents for me to have privacy also.

The tenth tent would have housed Tim and Skipper. But Tim insisted on pulling away from the group, curling up in his own little pup tent. And to everyone's disappointment, Skipper's parents had been afraid that if he came he'd catch a cold. For Skipper, fevers brought debilitating convulsions. So he had stayed home.

We stashed the first-aid equipment, the one folding cot, and Dave's C.B. radio in the extra tent. Frankie watched, whimpering, "What's gonna happen now?"

"Swimming and boating!" David called. "Meet you all on the dock."

"No! I can't!" Frankie seized my arm. His terror had to do with changing. The only time he went in the pool at camp was when he was wearing his bathing suit under his clothes, and he would pull his pants on over his wet swim trunks as soon as he left the water.

"We're all going to change, Frank." I unpeeled his fingers, which were gripping me so tightly they left marks on my arm. "You can use the first-aid tent for now. I'll be nearby."

José and Carlos raced to the dock. Adam, towel-cape flapping, ran behind them. Suddenly I heard Frankie screaming like a wounded soprano. Rodney stood in the doorway of the first-aid tent, pointing and laughing at Frankie. "Let's see what ya got down there, white cracker, think you so special—"

"Fag! Fag! Get outta here, black boogie fag!"

Rodney saw Richard approaching and scurried away, cursing Frankie.

"At least take the responsibility for bringing it on yourself," Richie said, pursuing Rodney.

Good for you, Rich, I thought. I liked the way he, and Bill and Ellen too, had learned to handle problems with the children.

On the girls' side of the campsite, Ellen was also running into trouble. There was no bathing suit in Maria's shopping bag. Gail abandoned the search party, tapping her head and telling Maria "You got chili 'stead of brains, girl!" Maria burst into tears.

Ellen checked through Maria's clothing, even looked in her bedroll, before tying the tiny, dark-haired child into her own extra bikini—so large on Maria the cups of the bra extended around to her shoulder blades. The bottom could only be secured by lacing the long top straps underneath it, like mini-pants with suspenders.

Rodney, himself still fully clothed, mocked Maria as she daintily picked her way over the pebbles. "Hey girl, I seen some funny bits—but Ellen's top on your mosquito-bite tits—"

"Rodney!" Ellen clapped her hand on her forehead.

But Maria didn't need a champion. She kept on walking, without missing a step. "If I wanted to be insulted, Rodney—Big Man—I would have stayed at home."

Billy, long, lean and freckled, walked Nathaniel, clutching Killer, to the water's edge. Nathaniel had been withdrawn since the search for the home of his mother's boyfriend.

"Rodney! Frankie! Hurry up!" I adjusted the shawl over Laura's plaster cast and spindly leg.

Frankie hesitantly emerged, his milk-white tummy rolling over the top of his emerald-green swim trunks. He held one handle of Laura's wheelchair the way a toddler clasps a baby carriage, while I pushed Laura down the bumpy path to the dock.

Rodney sauntered behind, thumbs hooked on the rear pockets of his skinny jeans, blue plastic comb riding high in his glinting Afro. He hadn't swum all summer, insisting he was allergic to chlorine. But surely he could enjoy the clear lake water.

"Ain't got no swim suit." He shrugged, suppressing a grin, and waved off Bill's offer to lend him some shorts.

Dave waited on the dock beside two stacks of orange life preservers. After I locked the brake on Laura's wheelchair, he reviewed the safety rules he'd printed on a chart: Everyone was to wear a life preserver. Three in a boat—one must be a counsellor. Fifteen-minute turns. Don't paddle beyond Dave's range of vision . . .

The children listened eagerly, and lined up to take turns. Both canoes, with Billy, Ellen and children, went gliding across the water. Dave swam a little way out behind them, counting strokes to establish rhythm for the oarsmen. Richard sat in the stern of the rowboat. Gail manned the oars. Trembling with fear and excitement, Maria perched in the bow, her black eyes gleaming, tiny body swallowed by the life preserver.

The other kids were strapped into life preservers and splashed in the deep water close to the dock. Frankie, Laura and Rodney stayed on the wooden platform.

I headed back toward them. Frankie was asking, "What's gonna happen next, Dave, after this?" then I heard Rodney snarl. "Here's what's gonna happen—"

There was a big splash and Frankie howled, arms and legs flailing as his body barreled over the dock into the water. His head bobbed to the surface almost instantly and Frankie rescued himself, dog-paddling valiantly with Dave at his side calling encouragement.

"That's what you get for callin' me names, honky!" Rodney roared, kneeling at the edge of the dock.

From the corner of my eye I saw Laura sweep the shawl from her lap and, limping on her cast, move up behind Rodney. Laura was walking! I watched transfixed, not believing what I knew would happen. And then Laura shoved Rodney right into the water.

Head first, he plummeted in and sank like a stone. Furtively Laura scurried back to her chair and bent to retrieve the shawl for her legs.

The kids in the boats clapped and cheered. "Yay, Laura!"

But Rodney didn't surface. I held my breath. Surely he could swim. Where was he? Why didn't he come up? I ran back along the dock, beginning to panic. "Get him, Dave! Help Rodney!"

Dave looked at me in alarm and dove underwater.

It was only seconds, but eternal seconds, before Dave surfaced with Rodney, who was spitting water, gasping, crying.

I pulled on Rodney's arms, Dave boosted his bottom then scrambled up to kneel beside him. All three boats came in. The children were very frightened and stared at Rodney, sprawled motionless on the dock, then at Laura, whose head was bowed.

"You're okay, Rodney," I said, my hand on his back. I felt his breathing, fast but steady.

Very slowly, he began to lift his head. Just enough to glance at Laura. "She—she can walk," he said faintly. A tear dripped off his nose onto a wooden plank.

"You really *can* walk, Laura!" Gail yelled from the rowboat, abandoning the oars to position her fists on her hips. "I seen you from the rowboat—"

"No you didn't!" Laura shrieked.

Ellie, Bill and I looked at each other in amazement. How could she deny what many of us had witnessed?

"I seen you too!" Maria squealed. "I seen you push on Big Man."

"I did too, Laura."

"Just a little! Only for a minute. Not very far!" She turned her head away.

"No, Laura." I took her chin in my hand, forcing her to face me. "If you can walk for a minute, you can walk for an hour."

She lowered her eyes. "No! I can't!" she whined. "I can't do it ever again. I only did it to get even."

"C'mon, Laura." Bill extended his hand. "Let us help you."

"Yes!"

"Get up!"

Laura began to raise herself, leaning on her trembling arms. Even Rodney stared. When she was almost standing, she swayed and collapsed in the chair. "There! You see! Now leave me alone!" She drew the shawl up to cover her face.

Humiliated and cold, Rodney leaned heavily on Dave and Richard, his arms around their shoulders. His toes barely touched the ground as they helped him up the hill to the first-aid tent, where Rich stripped off his soaking jeans, eased him into dry shorts and lowered him onto the cot. Dave covered Rodney with his old wool army blanket.

Rodney was almost asleep when Nathaniel dropped by to prove to Killer that Big Man hadn't drowned.

Outside, Adam circled the tent. "Splat! He hit the drink, but these wonder gloves managed to whisk him to safety! Shwooosh—K-pow!"

José helped Billy push Laura's wheelchair back to our campsite. Ellie, shaken as I was, stood at my side. "I don't understand it, Mom. How can a kid as young as Laura be such a master at manipulation?"

"Ellie dear, I'm as surprised as you are."

We'd planned to have the tug-of-war after swimming, but the kids emerged from their tents after changing clothes so subdued and lethargic that once the teams—Iroquois and Navahos—were chosen, the activity was postponed in favor of a nature walk.

"Watch for birds' eggs, animal tracks, rabbit holes," Bill instructed as the teams started off, Dave pushing Laura, Nathaniel carrying Killer. Millie Camp Dog pulled Tim, who held her by the collar. Adam Zocked! and K-k-k-powed! Frankie protested leaving me.

"Squaw stay here. Guard tepee." Dave winked, nudging Frank till he moved on his own.

"I'll find you as soon as Rodney wakes up," I called. But Rodney was still sleeping, curled like a baby, when they returned with their treasures—stones, egg shells, feathers. And surprising news from Nathaniel. When no one was watching, he'd released his snake in the woods. Nathaniel returned with Killer's jar, lidless and empty.

"I'm afraid of what this might mean, Mom," Billy said, watching Nathaniel slump dejectedly against a tree trunk. "Walking back from the woods he told me he thought about running in front of cars. Then the police would have to find his mother. And letting go of Killer. Could a kid as young as Nat feel suicidal?"

I worried, too. I knew that depressed children were sometimes victims of "accidents." We all agreed to keep close watch on Nathaniel.

Our next project was to paint Indian faces on each other. I sat beside Nathaniel and asked him about what he'd said but he assured me he only *thought* about running in front of cars. He wouldn't really do it.

The campers finally had their tug-of-war, but Rodney slept through it.

Frankie kept asking, "Now what? What's gonna happen next?"

"Cooking time!" I announced. "Everybody's gotta help—" I spun Laura, the tug-of-war referee, in her wheelchair, toward the picnic tables, and jogged across the clearing.

Gail chopped Spanish onions. Tim grated cheddar cheese. Diane peeled avocados. Adam cut up tomatoes. Maria arranged the food on paper plates, a colorful line-up on the picnc table. Carlos added a basket full of tacos. At last José, beaming proudly, carried the pan of steaming beef from the open fire to the table.

Maria demonstrated how to fill a taco. Everyone tried, except Frankie. "I can't eat! I can't eat without my mother."

Rodney still hadn't appeared. I tiptoed to the tent to check him through the window. He was finally awake.

He lay on his stomach, the microphone to Dave's C.B. radio close to his mouth. The intensity in his voice kept me riveted, silent.

"Dad. Calling Dad. This is Rodney, Dad. Also known as Sonny. Code Name: Big Man. Hey Dad—" His voice softened. "Listen Dad.

How you doin', Dad? This is Rodney, Dad, remember? I—I—n-need you, Dad. So when you comin' home? Momma tole me where you're at. In jail. I got troubles too, Dad, an' that's how come she tole me. I take stuff, too, see, an' if I get mad I push on people. But today I got pushed on. And Dad, I—I nearly drowned. So I—I need you Daddy—Dad. You hear me?" He put the mike to his ear and listened, before he spoke again. "Listen, Dad. Momma say you don't want me walkin' in your shoes. But if I go to jail you'd be there. Right, Dad?" he listened again. "Right Daddy? Dad—Dad? Help! Daddy! Help! Shit! How come you don't never answer!" He threw the microphone across the tent.

"Rodney." He jumped when I touched his blanket.

"What you want?" he whispered, clearing his throat.

"I'm sorry about your dad. I heard you talking."

The dog, who had trailed me, tried to nuzzle closer to his buried face.

Silence. Rodney circled his arm around the dog, now standing on her hind legs. "You know about it, too, ole scum dog?"

"Do you write to your father, Rodney?"

"Uh-uh."

"I've worked with people in prison. Most of them hope to hear from their kids."

"Why doncha report me?" he interrupted. "Call the cops for me pushin' Frankie and—and—"

I waited.

He turned his head to Millie and whispered hoarsely into her ear, "For takin' Billy's wallet. I—I'm sorry. Sorry Billy didn't go to Boston."

"Maybe you can tell him that, Rodney. I bet it might make Bill feel better."

The other kids were relieved to see Rodney. And he knew how to make an entrance. Sauntering over to the fireplace he drawled, "I'll take a steak. Pink throughout."

But it was a shadowy version of Big Man who nibbled on his taco without an ethnic comment and glanced occasionally at Bill.

Bill was sitting with Nathaniel, who'd tried to return to the woods alone to search for Killer. He wept into the empty jar.

Frankie, still whining, hadn't taken a bite when Ellie removed the aluminum foil from a dessert that was a complete surprise.

"Happy UN-Birthday, everyone!" She grinned. "Since we won't be together for each other's birthdays, I made us all an UN-birthday celebration!"

"Wooo-eeee!"

"Way to go, Ellie!"

Gail and Maria hugged her.

As the song began, "Happy unbirthday to me, Happy unbirthday to you . . ." Frankie had to wail louder to be heard.

"It's gonna be a long night, Ma," Richie murmured.

"And let's not forget Skipper. Happy unbirthday to Skipper, too," Ellie said, slicing through the chocolate frosting.

I looked around the group, suddenly realizing Skipper wasn't the only person missing. Where was Diane? I hadn't seen her since we finished cooking.

"Oh, she's over there," Laura said. She pointed to the grove of pine trees.

Gail nodded. "Kissin' her honey."

"What?" Dave and I stared at each other before we followed Rich into the woods. Diane and a boy were hugging each other behind a big tree.

"Here comes Tonto," the boy said, looking over her shoulder at Rich, who was festooned in Indian headdress and war paint.

"A whole tribe—" He grinned, seeing Dave and me.

"You're expected to stay with the group, Diane," I began.

She glared at me through hooded eyes. "So what? It wasn't my idea to come camping."

"My name's Pete." The boy took over. "I didn't know she hadda stay with the group. That's cool. I'll see you later, Diane."

"You know each other?" I wondered if they had just met in the woods.

"From school."

"Well, I'm glad you understand."

"Yeah. Sure." He sped away. We were left with a surly young woman.

And also with Frankie threatening to vomit if we didn't call his mother. Billy walked him to the toilet and the rest of us went out on the dock to watch the glorious coral sunset reflect on the water. The first star came out. And then it was dark. The kids collected sticks for a campfire. Frankie grew more frantic. "You fools! You idiots! One of you—right now—call my mother! If you don't, I'll have you all arrested."

Maria's lower lip quivered. Laura turned away, biting her lip. Nathaniel locked his arms around his knees and looked at the ground. I wanted to quiet Frankie before his anxiety spread further.

"Get away from me, witch! Nobody can help me now."

But he grew calmer and I uttered a silent prayer of thanksgiving.

The children scattered, hands cupped to catch fireflies, all but Frankie and Nathaniel, who sat on the grass beside me, rocking Killer's empty jar.

"The kids where I live do that," Frankie said, watching. "The kids in my neighborhood—they have a lot of fun."

"Do you go out with them?"

"No." He shook his head. "You know I'm too nervous. You know that I couldn't do that."

"No, Frank. I know that you can! You can control your nerves."

"God damn it!" He picked up a rock and threw it. "You know I really can't!"

"You're wrong. And do you know how I know you can?" I asked slowly, deliberately. "Throwing that rock was the kind of explosion I've seen you have before, just when you're ready to take another risk."

Frankie toyed with another rock. But he'd cocked his head to listen.

"Yup—that's how you get rid of your tension when you're about to try something new."

In no time he was running with the others.

He hadn't caught a firefly but he kept trying, leaping awkwardly, landing heavily—once on his broad-beamed bottom. Suddenly Gail streaked out of the woods toward the campfire. "Stay away from there!" She pointed, gasping. "Keep back! I seen a skunk!"

"Shh! Stand still! Don't scare him."

Across the meadow the kids froze like statues in a garden.

"Here he come!" someone screamed.

Dave turned his powerful flashlight on the animal stepping gingerly from the woods.

Camp Dog! From neck to tail, someone had streaked her black coat white.

As she came closer and Tim ran to embrace her, we saw that she had something writhing, dangling from her mouth.

"Killer!" Carlos shouted. "C'mere, Nathaniel! Camp Dog found Killer!"

Since I was far from being an expert on snakes, I couldn't have sworn it was Killer. But Nathaniel accepted the miracle without hesitation. And perhaps it was unlikely that Millie would have found another snake with Killer's markings.

Nathaniel seemed dazed. Carlos, José and Rodney helped him reline the familiar jar with fresh grass.

Others clustered around Millie, heaping lavish praises as they stroked her. The bravest . . . the smartest . . . They paused to sniff the cloud of dust rising from the dog.

"Baby powder!"

"Who'd baby-powder Camp Dog?" Carlos frowned, both fists readied.

"Don't worry. I'll fix her." Tim ran for his knapsack. "Get some food so she'll stand still. Poor little Camp Dog . . . who'd do that to dear little Camp Dog . . ." he fretted, returning with his hairbrush.

José scooped leftover meat onto a fresh paper plate. Frankie brought it to Millie cautiously. "C'mon girl. Eat."

A ring of children anxiously surrounded the dog. There was mounting concern when she failed to nibble.

"Maybe the person what done it to her hurt her."

"Maybe she's just embarrassed."

"Please eat, Camp Dog," Frankie whispered, pushing the plate even closer. "You could die if you don't."

"Maybe she will if she sees you eating." Ellie got the plate she'd fixed for Frankie.

Tim brushed out Camp Dog. She began to gobble her supper as Frankie, squatting beside her, bit into his taco.

Beautiful multicolored faces glowed around the crackling campfire. Billy, on guitar, led the singing.

rhythmic dance before Rodney poked his head from his tent. And then Carlos. José. Frankie and Nathaniel. Adam, who'd hidden behind a tree, caught Billy by the fringe on his vest and hopped awkwardly beside him. Billy winked at me. Adam had no trouble linking up with this fantasy.

Richie's drumming reached fever pitch. Then suddenly silence. A powerful stillness. Only the crackling and snapping of the fire.

Then a gentler drumbeat began. "Chief show you spearhead." By the flickering firelight Dave displayed the Indian artifacts he'd collected, telling a simple story about each one.

Rodney crept closer. The other boys followed, except for Tim. His tent flap remained closed.

"Be right back, dear." I freed myself from Gail, whose head was on my shoulder. She moved to Ellen, who was holding Maria.

"Knock-knock, Tim. I want you to see the show—"

"Leave me alone, Eleanor. Can't you tell I'm asleep?"

"But Tim, you did so much planning to make this camp-out successful. Why miss the show?"

"Because"—a tiny muffled voice—"something's happened and it's all my fault."

"Okay. But why don't we talk about it? Closing people out isn't a solution, Tim. I think you deserve a solution."

"Uh-uh. I tried to stop them, but they kept on fighting and—and my father walked out."

"That's your fault?"

"I shoulda stopped them."

"I can't yell above the drum," I said, "I'm coming in." But that was physically impossible. The best I could do was kneel and poke my head in the tiny tent.

Tim was curled up, under a patchwork quilt, his eyes squeezed shut. "Tim"—I wiped his sweaty forehead—"you're taking too much on yourself. You want to help your parents, but no kid can be as powerful as that."

"I think they were fighting the day I was born. Now everybody in our house is fighting. Even the dog and the cat."

"Oh Timmy, I'm sorry. There are some things we just can't control. Even things we wish for so much. Know what? Wishing can't make parents stop fighting." I looked across the grass at Richie, who was putting so much energy into beating the drum. Beads of perspiration glistened on his dark mustache. The red and yellow zigzags painted on his temples had begun to streak down his cheeks.

Rich was the wisher in my group—the one who hoped till the end there'd be no separation.

"Anyway, Eleanor, I don't feel like socializing. I'd rather be left alone."

"I won't argue with you Tim, but I'll be outside if you want me."

Perhaps he thought I'd left when he finally poked his head out. He had put his glasses on. He sat beside me without speaking.

The children were all wide-eyed as Dave ended his performance by holding up a long clay object. "Chief Goodhope ask all his people to join him passing pipe for peace."

Richie continued beating softly on the tom-tom. Bill and Adam weaved to the rhythm. Rodney straightened his shoulders and stepped forward.

"Peace, brother, peace." Dave said, drawing on the empty pipe. He handed it cautiously to Rodney, who put on a momentary show of coughing as he held the stem to his lips, then somberly repeated "Peace, brother, peace" and offered it to Nathaniel.

Ellie's turn. "Peace to all my sisters and brothers."

"Hurry, Tim." I pulled him to the circle. "Peace. To all the Hopewell Indians." I placed the pipe in Tim's shaky hands. "Peace," he whispered.

"Any boys around?" Gail stuck her head and naked chest out the door of her tent. "Whew! No one lookin'!" She disappeared slowly.

"Eleanor!" Maria wailed, "I lost my cross! And I can't go to sleep without it 'cause it keeps away the devil!"

We organized a fruitless search by flashlight, then I sat on the tent floor, to comfort Maria, quaking in her sleeping bag. "Now I won't be able to talk to Jesus."

"Sure you will dear. Talk to him in your prayers."

"Nombre del Padre del Hijo y . . ." She crossed herself.

Ellie helped Billy put Adam to bed, Adam's war whoops from the darkened tent echoing across the lake.

Rich settled Frankie. Dave and I made final rounds with his flashlight.

"G'night, Gail!"

"G'nght, Laura!"

"Hey—Carlos."

"G'night!"

"Gosh, we sound like the Waltons."

"Shhh. Here come Dave."

When all the kids were in bed, Dave and I strolled to the end of
the meadow for a last look at the shimmering water. Rodney's voice
carried through the still night air.

"Hey, Nat. You think Eleanor and Dave make love?"

"Uh-uh. I ain't never seen them."

"Maybe he's a homo."

"Huh!" Dave grunted indignantly.

"What's that?"

I had to stifle a giggle.

"Jeez, Nat. How can I talk to you! Look, you know what happens
in a seduction . . ."

"Su—what?"

"Where you been, kid? When a dude give a woman a baby—that's
seduction."

"Oh." Nathaniel yawned. "How long do it take?"

"Hmmm," the expert pondered, "anywhere from—ah—a couple
a seconds to—ah—never. Jeez"—his voice faded—"someday I'd like
to look at some girl's tits."

"Guess I'll have to talk with Rodney," Dave whispered.

"Not before I do! What a little chauvinist."

We walked back toward the fire, listening as we passed each tent.

". . . I love all kinda boys," Gail was telling Maria. "Hey, 'member
that game we useta play—you know. You're the good good kid and
I'm the wicked mother? Let's make pretend that I just spanked you
and I pushed you into your bed. And now I'm drinkin' up my beer
and huggin' with one of my honeys."

Rich, Bill and Ellen appeared from tents where they'd been waiting till the children fell asleep.

We sat around the campfire, talking, humming, listening for

sounds from the kids. Finally we admitted we were all exhausted, too, and tossed more sticks on the campfire before we said good-night.

"See you at morning circle." We hugged each other.

I'd never camped before. But I fell asleep moments after crawling into the slippery nylon sleeping bag, unaware that the fire was slowly dying.

It was pitch black inside and out when the child's screaming woke me. I groped for a flashlight and scrambled barefoot over the dewy grass.

Maria. The cries came from Maria. She'd dreamed about the devil turning into a baby stealer. She saw his big eyes, staring through the window, and woke up as he put out his arm to grab her.

I rocked her, listened to her dream, told her about the Indians who instructed their children to dream the same dream again, only give it a better ending.

"You mean like I could scare the devil?"

"Sure! Like that! Or you punch him in the nose when he peeks in your window."

Maria giggled.

"Look, girl." Gail, her headful of tiny braids matted flat, sat up rubbing her eyes. "Don't ya understand? If you didn't get no bad nightmares, you might never get no good dreams!"

I tiptoed out, thinking Gail and I were the only persons Maria's cries had wakened. But Dave stood in the entrance to Diane's tent, beckoning me with his flashlight. I poked my head in beside his shoulder and was shocked to find four eyes glaring back. Diane and the boy she'd met in the woods.

"What's going on?" I demanded.

"That." Dave flashed the beam on an empty wine bottle, then handed me the driver's license he'd taken from the boy. "You'll get it back when I see your parents tomorrow."

"Yes sir." The boy fled, presumably to his family's campsite.

I turned to Diane. "How could you violate our trust?"

"What are you gonna do about it, Eleanor?" she sneered. "Tell my mother? Well, ya can't cause she's in Spain with her boyfriend. Tell my father? You'll hafta call up every bar in the city to find him. I know! You could go home and write a book about it."

"I know what I'd say about you. A fine girl letting herself act tough and wise."

I moved my sleeping bag and spent the night between the sullen girl and the entrance to her tent.

"What your parents do doesn't excuse your actions, Diane. Let's be honest with each other from now on."

"Psst—hey, Eleanor—why doncha get up?"

I lifted my head. It was still dark, but grayish enough to see the shadows of Frankie's chunky outline as he beckoned to me. "We could start the breakfast."

It was mid-August, but I needed three sweaters and two pairs of socks in the early morning chill.

Frankie was delightful. Full of confidence. Thrilled with camping.

"Notice anything different?" He glanced at me.

Different! In every way!

"Gosh," he went on, "you always had plenty to say when I didn't useta change my clothes! Now I get all dressed by myself and you don't say nothin'!"

"Oh, Frankie, congratulations!"

He squirmed away from a hug.

"I don't cook gourmet meals like spaghetti or hot dogs"—Frankie heaped fresh coals in the fireplace—"in fact, I don't cook at all. But I'd like to learn."

"Hey!" Rodney staggered from his tent, naked except for Billy's white shorts, and the blue sleeping bag draped on his shoulers. "You guys woke me up in the middle of my juiciest dream."

Dave, jogging by in his red and gray track suit, caught Rodney's dour expression. "You in some kinda depression?"

"Think it's still 1929, Dave?" Frankie grinned.

Rodney banged a wooden spoon on the bottom of the frying pan, to waken the other campers.

Ellie and I pulled shorts over Laura's leg cast. Laura did little to help, but at least she was truthful. "When I get ready at home I go as slow as I can. I like to make my mother yell. I do it every morning."

By seven-thirty everyone had washed and dressed. We clustered around the flagpole in front of the community house to sing "The

Star Spangled Banner" while a uniformed forest ranger hoisted a flag up the tall white pole.

> *. . . land of the fre-e-e-e-e
> and the ho-o-o-o-me of the brave.*

"Proving once again, folks," Frankie said, saluting the fluttering banner, "that America is still off key."

Walking back to finish cooking, I asked him what made him so different here.

"Well . . . uh . . . see"—Frankie hesitated, his eyes far away—"my mother's really the one who's scared. But when I'm with her it rubs off on me. Here," he said looking around, "here it feels different. At home, whatever way my mom feels, I feel that way too."

I thought of all the anxiety he'd had in anticipation. Even Rodney's shoving him into the pond had proven a breakthrough for Frankie.

After clean-up, he tied on an orange life preserver, and jumped off the dock, eyes squeezed shut, arms around his chunky legs, cannonball style.

But Rodney shook when Dave insisted he'd have to overcome his fear of water. He was furious and cursed at Dave, then fell into silence. Finally Dave was able to negotiate with him. Rodney would go in—to his knees—if Rich would take him someplace where no one else could watch.

I canoed with Nathaniel and Adam. "Splat! K-pow! Sit tight, gents!" Adam clutched both sides of the delicate boat. "Super-shrink will get us through."

Before we returned the life preservers to the little boathouse, Rich had Rodney floating on his back.

By eleven, everyone was dressed to go home, although one of Maria's socks was blue and the other yellow.

We folded the tents while Dave went to talk to the parents of the boy he'd found with Diane.

The campers dragged tents, sleeping bags and cartons back to the cars. Maria helped me box the leftover food. She hadn't found her cross. "Could you come to the project tonight, and stay in my room with me—and then when I scream you'd be right there?"

. . .

"So how do you like camping?" Billy grinned, ready to lead the circle of kids in a final song.

"I like it so much"—Gail grinned, traces of yellow warpaint still highlighting her rich dark skin—"so much it makes my smilers hurt."

"Do we have to go home?" Frank whined. "Why can't we stay another night?"

"Dy-no-mite! Hey, Rich . . ."—Rodney nudged my son—"me an' Nate need another night to try our plan. I was gonna wake up in the middle of the night screamin' 'Ellen! Ellen!' And then when she come runnin' in I'd tell her I'm too scared to sleep all alone."

"You sly thing, you!" Frankie beamed, forgetting his scowl.

Dave walked toward us with a big white tin of baby powder.

"The evidence!" Tim's jaw dropped.

Dave went right to Diane. "The young man says it's yours."

"Diane!"

"Poor Camp Dog!"

Gail and Maria backed away from Diane.

"You done that . . ."

"Uh-uh. Jim did!"

"She's the one what gave him the powder."

"Guess no one here can take a joke." Diane's voice trailed off.

"It wasn't funny to Camp Dog," Tim said as he stroked Millie, "was it?" He kissed the dog's black nose.

"Look. I'm sorry, okay?"

Silence.

"I'm sorry." Diane put her face against the dog's. Millie lifted her paw till it rested on Diane's hand.

Billy strummed the opening chord.

> So long. We've packed up our tents now.
> 'Bye bye. It's been fun to camp here . . .
> but we gotta go rolling along . . .

It was after two and Diane's maid still hadn't come to get her. I was sitting in the kitchen with Diane when Barry called from the clinic.

He was pleased with my interest in Day Treatment and thought I was well qualified to direct the program.

"The funding we were promised is already up in the air because of federal cutbacks." Barry sounded tired. "The governor's sending out teams to reassess the county's health needs. I can't make the meeting. If you'd represent Day Treatment, I won't take it as a final commitment, though I wish I could. We're already getting referrals."

I called goodbye to Diane as Barry was still talking.

My kids and I had what was left of the weekend to decide the fate of all our belongings. I knew I couldn't store the history books and Richie's drums, Ann's closetful of old purses, jewelry boxes, toys she'd found in thrift shops, Ellie's paintings and sculptures, the awards she'd won riding horses, basketballs, bowling balls, Billy's amplifiers and guitars, and God knows how many dog-eared copies of *Playboy*.

I tackled Ann's room. Three piles: keep, Goodwill, and throw away. African masks, anthropology books, poems . . . Each time I brought a box down the stairway I'd meet Rich, Bill or Ellie carting treasures or a garbage bag of junk.

By seven P.M. we'd lined the front hall with bulging cartons. I called a halt and offered dinner at the Chinese restaurant. The budget seemed unimportant. Richie would be off to Korea in less than a week.

He tried to serve us with chopsticks—unfortunately for the tablecloth.

We grew silly, giggly, talking about things we'd found in the cleanup.

Toward the end of the meal, Richie cracked a fortune cookie. "What if it doesn't have a fortune? Ah, it does." He withdrew the folded paper. "Beautiful girl await you in Korea."

"Rich!" Ellie peered over his shoulder. " 'Life is change. Change with it,' that's what it really says!"

Suddenly we all stopped talking. One of those silences too meaningful to be broken.

Rich finally cleared his throat. "We had fun as a family, didn't we?"

"We've laughed together again," said Bill. "We still are a family."

27

Diane was right. Dave couldn't contact either of her parents. The maid said her mother was due home in a week. No answer at the father's apartment.

But Laura's parents agreed to a meeting Sunday evening.

They both had trouble believing that we'd seen her walk. "Are you sure?"

Laura slumped in her wheelchair, shaking her head in furious denial.

"Well, why would she refuse to try again?" her father said challengingly to Dave and me.

"Ask Laura."

"Honey"—he reached for her hand but the girl pulled away—"I don't understand. You were so brave in the hospital. A real little soldier."

"I was not!" she spat. "Real soldiers get guns. If they gave me one"—she made a pistol of her index finger and held it to her eye—"I would've shot all them nurses and doctors."

"Don't talk that way!" her mother slapped her wrist.

Tears dribbled down her cheeks. Laura pulled up the shawl on her legs to wipe them away.

"What do you have to cry about?" Mrs. Burgman's voice rose. "We're the ones who ought to be crying." She nodded toward her husband.

"Then why didn't you?" Laura shrieked. "How come you smiled when I went to get the operation? You knew they'd hurt me!"

The puzzled couple stared at their daughter. David glanced at me and waited.

"I saw you!" Laura pointed a shaky finger. "I looked back when they wheeled me away. And both of you were laughing."

"Honey—" Her parents rushed to her side. "Laura . . . we fought so hard not to cry then, so you wouldn't be upset. The minute they rolled you away our eyes were full of tears. You should have seen us—"

"Like—like now," her mother sniffled.

"So the kid was holding out on her parents." Dave glanced out the window as her father folded the wheelchair into their car. "A real sit-down strike to punish them for what she didn't understand. Well," he shrugged, "I guess if families knew more about communication we wouldn't be having Camp Hopewell."

Bill and Ellen asked their friends Bob and Sharon to help at camp on Monday. I went to the Board of Education for the hearings on our kids' school placements. Rodney's began at 8 A.M. I expected to be back before camp was over. But all the meetings ran late. By the time I got home Ellie was hosing off the easels.

"Big news, Ma—Laura came to camp on crutches! She walked all over the yard! And Skipper's mom asked if I'd babysit till it's time to go back to school. She says he calls for 'Eh-yee.'" Ellie grinned. "Oh, and Frankie doesn't believe you went to meetings. He told us all that you're 'camp phobic.'"

We'd been having pleasant meals together. I felt left out and puzzled when my kids drove off before I started supper. A hurried story about saying goodbye to friends with Richie.

I read in the living room, a record playing in the background. It was almost ten when I heard their footsteps in the hallway.

"Wow! You really have been packing!"

Ann's voice! I dropped the book. My God—it was Ann!

I ran, stumbling, laughing, crying to hug her. I held her close, then pulled away to see her before we hugged again.

Ann was bony, freckled, deeply tanned, wearing a blue African galabiya. Even so thin, her face was lovely.

"Rich—Bill—Ellie" They stood behind me, grinning. "How come you didn't tell me?"

"We didn't know yourselves till Annie called from the airport. Then we decided to surprise you."

"You did. You succeeded."

Excitement mounted Wednesday as kids prepared for Awards Day, putting finishing touches on the books they'd written, the sculptures, collages and paintings.

Gail, Maria and Laura dressed the papier mâché puppets they'd constructed in Ellie's art group. Rich drilled the boys on precision basketball moves. Rodney named the group the "Hopewell Hot Shots." Frankie hadn't told his family he swam now. Dave agreed to let him surprise them the next day. Billy's kids worked on skits and invited me to watch a run-through.

Tim bowed from the waist to announce his production: "The War of Kids Against Grown-ups."

He and Frankie maneuvered dozens of green plastic soldiers around so that the entire adult army died in the first assault. About half of the kids survived to turn on one another until the last one fell.

Nathaniel played a final airplane game, asking me to co-pilot, thereby demoting Killer to front-row traveler. The wings fell off and the motors caught on fire, but for the first time the pilot maintained control and brought the plane down safely. I reached for Nathaniel's hand as he wiped the sweat from his forehead.

Richie caught my attention by whistling softly and pointing toward the hedge. I walked quietly toward the bushes and bent to see. Diane crouched underneath, an amber liquor bottle in her hand glinting in the sunlight. She tilted the bottle to her lips, then tucked it under the shrubs and scurried across the yard to the barn. Shocked, I rushed to confront her.

I found her putting on her bathing suit. "Oh no, you're not going swimming."

"All ri-i-i-ght." Her face got red. "What's wrong with you?"

"I'm okay, Diane. You can't swim because you've been drinking." I held her chin. Her eyes avoided mine. "What are you doing to yourself, Diane?"

"What's bugging you?" Her whiskey breath hit my face.

"What's bugging me is watching a lovely kid who's wrecking herself."

"If you tell my mother I'll run away! I swear it! She has problems of her own." Her voice rose. "She doesn't need trouble from you!"

"Trouble from me?" I caught her fist. "Or from you?"

"Anyway she's not home. You won't be able to reach her, 'cause she's off on a trip with her boyfriend."

"Then one of us will call your father. Will it be you or me?"

"You can." She looked away. "He won't give a damn."

"I couldn't come up tomorrow. My agency's sponsoring an outing at the Westchester Golf Club."

"I wasn't thinking of tomorrow, Mr. Woodruff. I don't intend to let Diane go home today without my talking to one of her parents."

Diane waited all afternoon by the pool, brooding and surly. She wouldn't come to closing circle. When the others left, I cancelled my clinic appointments.

Mr. Woodruff arrived at four-fifteen, having taken a city taxi forty miles. He was about six-foot-four with slicked-back hair, bushy eyebrows, a long nose and puffs of purple flesh under ice-blue eyes.

"Walt Woodruff." He shifted his jacket to the other arm. "What's this about?" He looked concerned.

"I don't want her to hurt you, Dad," Diane said, clinging to his arm.

"What is it, baby?" He loosened his tie then reached for her hand. "You know old Dad's not gonna be mad."

"Eleanor caught me drinking."

Puzzled, he looked at me. "Today and on the weekend," I said. "Mr. Woodruff, we're really concerned."

The back of his shirt was damp. "Baby, baby, why? Why would you want to do that?"

Diane looked pleased. "I guess"—she glanced into her father's face—"I guess because—because of you and Mom. Because you're divorced."

He crumpled as though she had struck him, his fist against his forehead. For seconds we heard only his heavy breathing.

"You accept that, Mr. Woodruff?" I asked. "That your divorce justifies her drinking?" I felt Diane's angry glare.

"I—uh—I guess I've always blamed myself for any troubles my girls had. Oh sure, I tried to put it on their mothers. But maybe her sister wouldn't have gotten into drugs if I hadn't had to leave."

"HAD to leave?"

"Even our marriage counselor agreed. It was the only way. My relationship with her mother was vicious. One giant mistake right from the beginning."

His daughter folded her arms and stared at me, smirking as though her father's pain vindicated her behavior.

"So the girls have punished you ever since?" I asked.

Diane recoiled, her mouth wide open.

"I never thought of it like that." Her father's expression mirrored Diane's surprise. "Maybe—maybe—that's what's going on."

"Dad, it's not because of you!" Diane kissed his cheek. "It's Mom and all her crazy boyfriends."

In the hour before Rich drove him back to the train, Diane and her father worked out an agreement. He'd return for Awards Day and participate in future family meetings. She wouldn't drink for at least four more years, until her eighteenth birthday.

He kissed and hugged his daughter. "I trust you, baby. You know your old Dad trusts you."

I hurried inside to spend some time with Ann. But she was still asleep when I left for the Governor's hearing at the high school, my first official act in connection with Day Treatment.

The hundred or more who met in the lobby were herded into groups, then twenty-seven of us shuffled off into a classroom. A balding, paunchy man erased algebra equations from the blackboard and asked about our concerns.

I was the first to raise my hand. Holding yellow chalk in his nicotined fingers, he wrote "Day Treatment." Twenty-six more needs were identified before he made the announcement. We were expected to choose the six most deserving programs.

A shouting match followed, a contest between human services, until a Hispanic woman denounced the procedure as demeaning. She left the meeting, and most of us followed.

28

—Laura! Closing circle! C'mon outta the barn!

—I'm not comin' till I finish cryin'.

—Why should she cry? Dave danced with her! He didn't dance with me.

—Hey, let's make pretend this camp is just beginning.

—Yeah! Let's pretend we're all just startin' at this crazy little stink camp.

—Well, me—I don't want the summer to be over. I'm afraid to go back to school.

—Mmmm. I feel like that too. I don't have any friends there.

—How do you know?

—Valentines. I wrote twenty-eight. I only got one.

—S-o-o-o you must got one friend!

—Miss Wiener. Little Camp Dog, where are you?

—I'm never going back, 'cause even if I tried to, all the kids would ask me questions. Like where was I all last year.

—Say you went to Europe, Frankie.

—Uh-uh. Some kids are so rich they've already been to Europe. They'd ask him what he seen there.

—Anyway, Frank, your mother used to you bein' her baby, so you shouldn't go changin' that too fast.

—I won't. Don't worry.

—At my school some kids call me retard. That's how come I take things. I ain't no retard when I snatch stuff.

—I get called names also. There you are, little Camp Dog! When I'm a paleontologist I won't need people.

—I seen a doctor on TV hypnotize a guy to make him nicer. He done like this . . .

—Hey, keep you fuckin' hands to youself!

—But what if the doctor done it backward? Hypnotize Big Man, an' made him pay attention to the kids insteada the teacher?

—He wouldn't, Maria.

—Put Killer's jar down!

—Who'd wanna touch it, selfish!

—That doctor at the Guidance Center, he thinks I'm a nut.

—Well, you really was one, Frankie, when you useta scream for your momma.

—So! I still miss mine. Sometimes.

—I'll always want my father.

—Our father's nicer now. He's tryin' to do what Jesus wants.

—He tried it before—but it didn't work the first time.

—Even when I'm a mother, I'll bring my kids to Camp Hopewell. I have a right to come back, 'cause this year Skipper got all the attention.

—Oh sure, Laura, sure!

—Pee budder?

—Shhh! He heard you.

—Hey, Eleanor, after camp t'morrow, can we lock up the barn— so no one else can use it? It belongs to us, don't it?

29

We sat at the kitchen counter writing out certificates for the kids before we began our private staff celebration. Grilled red snapper, caught and cleaned by David. Toasts to Camp Hopewell with chilled rosé wine. The party turned into a jazz session with Ellie at the piano and Dave on my clarinet.

Ann and I listened from the kitchen. She read to me from the diaries she'd kept on her trip. Details of conversations and impressions. ". . . a country full of people caught in transition, struggling to move into modern times. Yet having, I believe, better survival mechanisms, more support for one another than our society offers . . ."

"It must have been what I needed all along, Ma, what I hoped to find by going away." She closed the book. "Methods of dealing with stress. I felt so much pressure at school. I'm not sure why. Me. Our family. Our society. I don't know . . ." Her voice trailed off.

"Annie"—I took her cold hand in mine—"I hope with all my heart that you feel better now."

30

Rich, Bill, Ellie and I had juice on the porch at seven in the morning. We'd all awakened with the same concern. What if it rained on Awards Day? But we were lucky. Another warm sunny morning.

Rich set up his drums on the porch. Bill worked on connecting a microphone to his amplifier for Ann, who'd promised to announce the prizes, freeing staff to mingle with guests and children.

Ann had yet to meet our campers. She'd slept through the days, though I heard her get up about midnight. Jet lag, she'd called it. "Please wake me by noon," she wrote on the note in the kitchen. "Lots of luck on Awards Day!"

Ellie and I set up the three dozen chairs we'd rented for eighteen dollars. Nine in a row on the grass in front of the porch. Dave arrived before eight, to vacuum the pool and section it into racing lanes with yards of white plastic clothesline.

Ellie draped a bed sheet over her paint-stained table in the art room of the barn, and arranged the children's sculptures with squares of paper telling the name of each artist. One might have guessed without a label that all the little animals connected to their mothers were Frankie's.

I placed the colorfully bound books the children had typed and illustrated on the picnic table. Gail's was the thickest. It was rich with stories about places she'd lived in and people she'd known there.

Rich left early to pick up the kids. It hadn't occurred to me they'd wear special clothes till Gail jumped out of his car in her sheer pink dress, her head full of ribbons. Rodney, in his fancy Fonz shirt, helped her drag a table from the porch across the grass to the entrance gate where they'd be waiting with a sign-in guest book for the visitors.

Nathaniel and the Hernandez kids Magic Markered "Guide" signs to pin to their worn but crisply ironed clothing.

Little Skipper wobbled from his mother's car dressed in royal blue shorts with a matching jacket. "Anybody home?" Rodney tapped on his helmet. "You look swift, kid." Skipper grinned and rocked his way down the driveway.

Diane, in the tight brown skirt and stack-heeled sandals she'd borrowed from her mother's closet, minced her way down the driveway till Rodney called for her to work on his committee.

Diane paused, hands on her hips, and slowly turned in his direction. "I always got the impression you really didn't like me."

"C'mon, girl," Rodney beckoned. "You gettin' to be one of my favorite enemies."

"Where oh where is dear little Camp Dog?" Tim, in his horn-rimmed glasses, white short-sleeved shirt and red bow tie, had brought a silver bow for Millie's collar. Laura laced crepe paper streamers through her crutches.

But who was the tall slim fellow in the man's-cut suit? Adam!

"Every last detail of this disguise," he said to his hand, "connects to the master plan through the most sophisticated electronic equipment known to Gallacticus." His voice rose. "They shoulda saved their money, mister." He opened and closed his hand like a mouth. "The chump looks like the jolly green giant! Sluuurp! K-pow!"

When Ceil Black drove up, followed by a carful of my co-workers from the clinic, I began to get nervous. I made a final check of the yard—red geraniums blooming at each corner of the flagstone terrace that edged the pool, sunbeams sparkling off the aqua water, children's bright paintings tacked to the wall of the barn, the grill, loaded with charcoal, waiting for the hot dogs at lunch time. The yard was ready. I hoped the kids were.

Nathaniel ran to Ceil's car to claim her as his special guest. "Git your butt back here, Nathaniel!" Gail roared. "She gotta sign her name with me and Big Man, or she ain't gonna see nothin'.'"

In the next half hour we greeted Mrs. Hernandez with her two youngest children, the Bennetts, Laura's parents and two of her brothers, three school social workers, Adam's aunt and uncle, his state worker, Nathaniel's aunt, Tim's and Rodney's mothers, Frankie's parents and several of the neighbors we'd invited.

So many people, Gail and Rodney lost track of who'd signed the guest book and they kept presenting it to people until it was time for Rodney to take part in the basketball demonstration.

There were ooohs and aaahs as the agile kids sank basket after basket, cheers when José flipped the ball through his legs to Rodney, who képt it bouncing behind his back till Carlos got behind him.

Rodney modestly raised his hands to halt the applause. "To our coach, From the Hopewell Hot Shots." They'd bought—at least I hoped they'd paid for it—a key chain for Richie.

Swimmers ran to get ready. Skipper, in yellow trunks and helmet, showed how well he'd learned to tread water. His father put his arm around his mother.

Gail outraced Maria, Tim and Nathaniel. Adam won the backstroke contest!

Then Dave called on Frankie, who'd run back to his old tree to hide.

"He's just doin' that for attention!" Laura yelled. Mrs. Cassone bit her lip, her face drained of color. Please come out, Frank, I prayed, afraid my going near him would aggravate his behavior.

"Maybe he'll swim for us later." Dave turned back to the crowd. "Now for the great underwater coin hunt!"

Bill and Rich threw fistfuls of pennies into the air. They swirled to the bottom of the water. And from every angle kids dove in to retrieve them. Rodney forgot he was allergic.

When every cent had been claimed, the excited kids scrambled out of the pool to compare their fortunes.

Hardly anyone noticed Frankie backing down the steps into the water. He took a deep breath and swam. One lap. Two. Five in all.

But Dave had been watching. "A record for Frank!" he shouted. Grinning, the chubby boy lumbered out of the pool, to be carefully dried by his shivering mother, and manfully thumped by his proud instructor.

At lunch time the children cooked and served. Hot dogs, fruit punch, macaroni salad. Dave and I were delighted with the response to the camp, especially from those workers who'd known our campers when they couldn't behave in group situations. ". . . sure don't look like the defiant kids we referred just eight weeks ago."

At one o'clock Ellie went inside to make sure Ann was ready. A long drum roll by Rich drew the crowd to the front of the house. We had more people than chairs. Some sat on the grass, others leaned on the fence. Our postman pulled up and turned off the motor to watch from his mail truck.

"Intro-ducing my sister Ann!" Rich called. "All the way from Africa to give out these awards!"

People gasped as Ann took her cue, wrapped sari-style in blue and white African batik, her eyes dramatically outlined with black Arabic kohl.

"Thank you! Thank you!" She was a natural master of ceremonies, smiling and comfortable. "I appreciate this chance to be with you. I'm sorry I haven't met you before, so when I say three would you call out your names? One—two—"

"Big Man!" "Gail!" Then a cacophony of sounds.

"All together now, and LOUDER!"

A groundswell. A roar. Followed by spontaneous laughter.

"Great! Now I feel as though I know you! So let's see who'll be getting the First Annual Camp Hopewell awards."

Gail's thumb found its way to her mouth. Rodney combed his hair. "Me?" Nathaniel raised his hand. José tried to sit up taller.

"For most improved swimmer . . ."

An even louder drum roll.

"Mr. Frankie Cassone!"

Frankie hesitated, then leapt up the three wooden stairs.

"Yeee-ay, Frank!"

Ann pumped his hand. Frankie turned purple. Whistles when she gave him the formal Certificate of Merit.

"A friend to all . . ."

Drum roll.

"Skipper Kerrigan!"

Ann glanced at me, startled, when Skipper waddled forward and tried to climb the steps on his hands and knees.

"The winner!" Her face paled as she bent to help him.

Skipper trundled from Ellie to his parents, flapping the gold edged paper, with a grin that spread to the sides of his helmet.

"The first time I ever won!" Gail shook her head in wonder when Ann announced best creative writer.

Rodney played it nonchalant. "Big Man's the name." He eyeballed Ann. But he delivered his basketball certificate directly to his mother.

Diane's father stepped out of a taxi just as Ann called his daughter's name. He stood at the fence clapping as Diane, head bowed, struggled to conceal her pleasure. Ann held her hand. "A special award, for efforts begun in the area of family relations."

"Most interested in fantasy and the supernatural!"

Billy winked at me during the drum roll. We'd had trouble deciding on a category for Adam.

"For excellence in promoting cross-cultural understanding . . . Carlos Hernandez!"

"*Gracias!*"

An award for every camper. And one still on the table.

"Well, that's it! Congratulations!" Ann applauded for the children.

"No!" "Look Ann!" "There's one more!"

Ann acted surprised.

Rich's long slow drum roll got louder throughout the announcement. "To the best four-legged explorer, best finder of snakes, best camp dog—*only* Camp Dog . . . Millie Craig!"

Holding on to her flea collar, Tim ran Millie up to the porch. Ann knelt to congratulate the dog. Millie lifted her paw and everyone applauded.

I thanked Ann. She'd added the perfect touch. I spoke briefly about our counselors, praising each one's skill and caring.

"Atta boy, Dave!"

"Yeah, Ellie!"

"Nice goin', Rich!"

"Go for it, Billy!"

We ended with our final closing circle. So many people were sitting on the grass, that we stretched from the barn to the pool. Shading my eyes, I spoke to the parents, foster parents, their children and mine, the social workers and friends.

"At closing circle, everyone's invited to comment. For me it's been a very special summer." Kids giggled as Millie slipped into the circle between Dave and me to parade from person to person like a show dog, pausing to relish caresses.

"She's saying goodbye," Tim kissed the dog's nose, "because she loves us."

"Then I'm with Camp Dog," Dave looked at the kids. "I'll miss you—every one."

"Dy-no-mite, Dave!" Rodney saluted with a double thumbs-up wriggle.

"Next year we'll bring our little sister."

"I never thought I'd get no award."

"I'm proud of my daughter."

"I thank the Blessed Virgin Mary for giving my children nice vacation."

Tim wrapped both arms around his legs, and closed his eyes to say it. His voice was squeaky, but loud. "I like Camp Hopewell more than, more than—dy-no-mite!"

"Right on, brother Tim!"

When we got to Gail, she leapt to her feet and dashed off toward the barn. "My puppet! I forgot to do my puppet!" Everyone watched her return, wearing the handmade puppet like a mitten.

"What's your name, girl?" Gail squatted in the center of the circle.

"Don't know." The puppet shook its brown-faced head.

"You dumb if you don't know what you name be!"

"I do! But I wanna change it. I want the same name as that mother."

"What mother? Where?" Gail looked around.

"That mother. See? I wanna belong to that one."

Gail hopped the puppet to Mrs. Bennett. "Could I be your girl? And live with you till I'm all growed up?"

"We'd—" Mrs. Bennett choked, "we'd like that—"

The puppet kissed them both. Mr. Bennett made space for Gail to sit between them.

Billy positioned his guitar so Adam could help him strum it. "Everybody ready?" His voice cracked.

I had trouble too, getting words past the lump in my own throat.

> *We got that Camp Hopewell feeling*
> *Deep in our hearts*
> *Deep in our hearts*
> *To sta-a-a-y—*

Working my way toward Dave, who stood at the gate, I paused for hugs with children, handshakes with adults, and to pick up three wet towels abandoned on the grass. Ellie lifted them off my arm and kissed me. "Great camp, Mom. Congratulations."

Richie gunned the motor on his old convertible and then got out to call his car pool. I watched him proudly, realizing how soon he'd be gone, how ready he was for his own life.

Billy said goodbye to Nathaniel. Then he and Ellie and I stood together as Rodney led the chain of kids past us up the driveway.

> *One and a two and a three four five—*
> *Camp Hopewell kids don't take no jive.*
> *Six and a seven. Eight nine ten.*
> *Bet your ass we'll be back again.*

"Not here," I said softly, "but we'll find a place—somewhere."
"One and a two—I'll bet you do." Billy nodded, grinning.

Elenor-I
hope you'll have
the camp a
Gen With the
Same peopile
☆ ♡ ☆
by For now From me

by for now from me
I Love you all
Gart ♡
P. S.
your
alwys
helping to

uted copies of the petition for her adoption to all her homeroom classmates.

Killer: Center School. Cared for by Nathaniel's classmates in large new aquarium.

Dave: Clincial Director, Center for Family Therapy.

Ann: Acting in a cabaret theater, New York City.

Bill: Museum School, Boston, Massachusetts. Video techniques.

Ellen: Fine Arts major, State University of New York at Purchase.

Richard: United States Peace Corps. Daechong, Chunbug Province, Korea.

Millie (Camp Dog): Died in her sleep. Buried at Camp Hopewell.

Eleanor: Clinical Director, Day Treatment Program, funded by the Stauffer Fund and State grants.

Yes, that's me. Sitting in the bedroom-study of my new apartment. Above the desk hangs a print that Billy gave me for Christmas, the picture by Millet of the peasant spreading seed. On the back he's written: "As you sow . . ."

I think of what we reaped together, Dave, my family and our Camp Kids. For all of us, some problems may be endless, but I hope we will remember the love and caring that we shared.

The trees outside are wintry bare now. Yet early this morning I saw a robin. A reminder to find a new location for the second summer of Camp Hopewell. I wish that we could run the camp through all four seasons. But then, like Nathaniel, I also wish that we could hear the grass grow.

ABOUT THE AUTHOR

ELEANOR CRAIG began working with children at twelve, when she and a friend ran a Saturday playschool for neighborhood children, charging thirty-five cents for the morning and subcontracting with a younger sister to take the children to the bathroom for five cents per journey. Since then she has worked in schools, clinics, and prisons as a counselor, teacher, and therapist and has visited facilities for special children in many countries, including China, Korea, and Japan. The author has a B.A. in Education and an M.S. in Counseling and has won an NDEA Fellowship for rehabilitation of emotionally disturbed children. She directed the summer camp described in this book for four years, and it continues to this day. Her other books include *P.S. Your Not Listening,* a best seller describing her teaching experience with troubled children, and *One, Two, Three: The Story of Matt, a Feral Child,* an in-depth portrait of the relationship between a needy mother and her deeply disturbed son. Her current work on behalf of children whose mothers are in prison is funded by a grant from the Coalition of Children and Youth.